# Sustaining Change:
# New Directions as Standard Practice

## Selected Papers from the 2002
## Central States Conference

Edited by
### Gale K. Crouse
### Sara K. Doering
### Carter E. Smith
University of Wisconsin-Eau Claire

**2002 Report of the**
**Central States Conference on the Teaching of Foreign Languages**

Publisher:        Lee Bradley, ❦
                  Valdosta State University
                  Valdosta, GA 31698

Printer:          Colson Printing Company
                  711 North Oak Street
                  Valdosta, GA 31601

ISBN:             1-883640-12-1

© Central States Conference on the Teaching of Foreign Languages
  Diane Ging, Executive Director
  Post Office Box 21531
  Columbus, OH 43221-0531
  Telephone 614-529-0109; facsmile 614-529-0321
  dging@iwaynet.net; http://centralstates.cc

7 2 3 L B 0 9 8 7 6 5 4 3 2 1

# Contents

## New Directions through Technology

## New Directions in Professional Development

# Review and Acceptance Procedures
# Central States Conference *Report*

The Central States Conference *Report* is a refereed volume of selected papers from the annual Central States Conference on the Teaching of Foreign Languages. Abstracts for sessions are first submitted to the Program Chair, who then selects the sessions that will be presented at the annual conference. Once the sessions have been selected, presenters are contacted by the editor of the CSC *Report* and invited to submit a manuscript for possible publication in that volume. Copies of the publication guidelines are sent to presenters who express interest in submitting a manuscript based on their presentation. Manuscripts that are submitted are read and evaluated by at least five members of the Editorial Board, individuals who are experts in the field of second language acquisition and foreign language methodology. Reviewers are asked to recommend that the manuscript (1) be published in its current form, (2) be published after particular revisions have been made, or (3) not be published. The editors make all final publishing decisions. The names and affiliations of the members of the Editorial Board are listed below.

The editors would like to point out that all website addresses (URLs) mentioned in the articles were fully functional at the time this volume went to press. This does not mean that those sites still exist or that the addresses given are still functional.

## 2002 CSC *Report* Editorial Board

### Editors

| | |
|---|---|
| Gale Crouse | University of Wisconsin-Eau Claire |
| Sara Doering | University of Wisconsin-Eau Claire |
| Carter Smith | University of Wisconsin-Eau Claire |

### Review Board

| | |
|---|---|
| Lee Bradley | Valdosta State University (GA) |
| Karen Cárdenas | South Dakota State University |
| Carol Ann Dahlberg | Moorhead, MN |
| Marilyn Gordon | Fremont, NE |
| John Janc | Minnesota State University, Mankato |
| Richard Kalfus | St. Louis Community College (MO) |
| Dave McAlpine | University of Arkansas at Little Rock |
| Gisela Moffit | Central Michigan University |
| Robert Terry | University of Richmond (VA) |
| Susan Villar | University of Minnesota |

# Preface

Kansas City, Missouri was the site of the Central States Conference on the Teaching of Foreign Languages, March 21-23, 2002. The theme of the 34th annual conference was **Sustaining Change**. This theme, along with its sub themes– *Teaching Tolerance and Understanding, Integrating Foreign Languages and Connecting to Other Disciplines,* and *Promoting Literacy via the Foreign Language Classroom*–is a timely one as we enter into another year of the new millennium. In the wake of the events of September 11, 2001, we as language professionals are challenged to work with students to help them become diverse learners and tolerant citizens of the world.

At this time in our history, it is even more important to work together with our colleagues in other areas of education to promote integrated learning and life-long skills. We are charged with educating a constantly-changing and ever-diverse group of students. Beyond the language itself, our focus must be teaching for tolerance as well as an appreciation and understanding of other languages, cultures, and ethnicities.

The conference featured two outstanding keynote speakers who addressed our need to *sustain change*. Mark Towers of Speak Out Seminars was the keynote speaker on Friday at the general session. His speech, *"Live With It, Lobby, or Leave,"* gave an informative yet humorous view of the challenges we face in education today. Dr. Protase E. "Woody" Woodford, an icon of our profession, addressed the attendees at the Saturday luncheon. His speech, *"Our Profession: What's Behind Us and What's Ahead?"* enlightened and entertained. Both speakers shared the very important message that we can indeed be agents of change and can thus impact the profession. Over 150 sessions and workshops provided conferees a wide variety of professional development opportunities.

The articles selected for this volume illustrate the strength of the Central States Conference and its dedication to explore new approaches and to meet new challenges in foreign language education– to set *New Directions as Standard Practice*.

–**Dena Bachman**
**2002 Program Chair**

# Board of Directors 2001 - 2002
# Central States Conference on the
# Teaching of Foreign Languages

# Introduction

## *Sustaining Change: New Directions as Standard Practice*

**Editors Gale Crouse**
**Sara Doering**
**Carter Smith**
University of Wisconsin - Eau Claire

The dichotomy evident within the title of this volume, *Sustaining Change: New Directions as Standard Practice,* highlights an essential nature of the teaching profession. Educators continuously strive for innovative ideas that allow them to "sustain change." This sustained change, however, becomes "standard practice" in the classroom and, in turn, provides opportunities for continued "new directions." The field of education has been criticized, at times, for reinventing the wheel, for returning to old ideas and simply dressing them up in new terminologies. Nonetheless, those who present this type of criticism fail to recognize one important point: the bedrock of our profession is the openness to reevaluate standard, accepted practices and to work towards an application of new discoveries and technologies to proven and successful pedagogical methods. Moreover, it is the professional call set forth by the *Standards for Foreign Language Learning in the 21$^{st}$ Century* (1999).

The articles in this volume reflect the idea of sustaining change and address this theme through a variety of perspectives. The first group of papers deals with the new directions that the use of technology in the language classroom offers both students and teachers. Robert Terry's article derives from an initial survey of states and their teacher licensure programs and the role, if any, that technology plays in teacher preparation and evaluation. He warns of the tendency to underestimate the potential uses of technology and advocates innovative and creative uses of technology in the teaching profession. Zoe Louton's article highlights the present state of many Distance Education programs and describes a two-state project that focuses on how distance education in the K-6 levels can enrich and extend curricula while enhancing the role of the classroom teacher. She presents the Iowa/Nebraska technology project as a model for future ventures. Finally, Jayne Abrate describes a year-long, unified project on Francophone culture for both secondary and post-secondary language classes. Her project incorporates the extensive use of the Internet in the language classroom and encourages and facilitates the development of the five Cs set forth in the *Standards*.

The second group of articles is closely related to the first in the attention given to technology and its application in the classroom. The positive roles that states can play in promoting and enhancing professional growth and in rewarding teachers who seek new directions in standard practices are profiled by Anne Nerenz and the group of Michigan educators working on the *Mich-I-Lifts* Project and by Stephen Brock and Vickie Scow in their description of Nebraska's STAR Award. Both articles provide models for other states to follow in the important efforts to expand teachers' professional horizons and improve the teaching profession.

The third group of papers responds to the *Standards'* goal to weave interdisciplinary elements into the teaching of a foreign language. Douglas Benson revives a call to recognize the study of literature and culture as integral elements of language courses and, most importantly, to integrate these elements in language study from the very beginning. His paper presents ample theoretical evidence as to why this is important as well as specific activities and ideas to utilize in the realization of this goal. Eileen Angelini's article on teaching the Holocaust in a French language course focuses on the importance of weaving together multiple disciplines (e.g., history, literature, politics, and culture) so that students can see that a language is not studied in an ahistoric vacuum.

The last group of papers takes these standard practices from the classroom and transfers them to the community, the greater society, and the world beyond the campus. They focus on ways to foment meaningful and direct interaction, both orally and in writing, through actual participation in the exchange of information and ideas among members of various cultures using the foreign language. Ruth Kauffmann describes the community-based curriculum she has established in her Spanish language courses. Her article relates how significant learning can take place by engaging students in the target language and culture through a curriculum that takes them out of the classroom and into the community. While ample opportunities for this type of learning abound in communities all over the United States for students of Spanish, this is not so for students of other languages. In his article, Jefford Vahlbusch studies the increasingly popular concept of service-learning and demonstrates that study abroad programs are an ideal venue for language learning and personal growth for students at the university level. He points out that a study abroad experience provides community-based, service-learning opportunities that may not be readily available here in the States. Finally, Susan Colville-Hall focuses on the importance of teacher development through a study abroad experience. Historically the vast majority of Spanish teachers who study abroad do so either in Mexico or Spain. She promotes the establishment of a Costa Rican program in the hopes of expanding the experiences and expertise of current and future Spanish teachers beyond a peninsular or Mexican focus.

What is common to all of these papers is a desire to utilize current, successful, standard practices as a springboard to new directions. They call others to examine current pedagogy, to evaluate new directions in the field of teaching foreign languages, and to sustain positive change that will impact both students and teachers. Whether the focus is promoting professional development, implementing new technologies in the classroom, weaving together curricular elements long considered separate, or bridging the gaps between classroom language study and its practical application in the greater society, our profession needs to sustain change and constantly strive for new directions. Only this way can we ensure the success and enjoyment experienced as one gains new knowledge, develops new skills, and pursues lifelong interests in other languages and cultures.

# 1

# Technology Competencies for Teacher Certification: A Survey of the States and a Challenge for Foreign Language Teaching

**Robert Terry**
University of Richmond

> The Digital Divide ... has never been about technology, but rather about people's understanding of what technology can do and the knowledge essential to apply it.
> –Mario Morino (2000)

## Introduction

Although Morino's statement may seem obvious, it is nonetheless true: The importance of technology in our everyday and academic lives is increasing. "Technology has become a powerful catalyst in promoting learning, communications, and life skills for economic survival in today's world" (International Society for Technology in Education [ISTE], 2000, p. xi). To address this situation, ISTE created the National Educational Technology Standards (NETS) project to develop national standards for educational uses of technology that facilitate school improvement in the United States. While the NETS project is concerned with Pre-K – 12 education and does not focus on any one discipline in particular, the broader and more long-range implications affect *all* phases of education, continuing through postsecondary to the adult and lifelong learner. Those statements made by ISTE in the NETS project are relevant to all educators, for learning does not stop at any particular and arbitrary point in one's academic career or life. The NETS and ISTE are encouraging educational leaders to provide learning opportunities that will produce technology-capable students (p. xi).

ISTE has developed standards-related documents that have been adopted by the National Council for Accreditation of Teacher Education (NCATE)[1] and that are used widely in the development and accreditation of teacher education programs in the United States. Two of these documents relevant to the survey that is the basis of this article are the unit guidelines describing essential conditions needed to support the use of technology in teacher preparation programs and the general standards for providing a foundation in technology for *all* teachers [emphasis added] (ISTE, 2000, p. xii).[2]

## Why the Survey?

Educational standards for K-12 in almost all 50states are now calling for technology competencies for students–competencies that will be measured; curriculum framework documents are advocating the inclusion and integration of technology in instruction across the curriculum. The *Standards of Learning for Virginia Public Schools* (SOL), which were adopted in 1995, for example, "emphasize the importance of instruction in four core subjects–English, mathematics, science, and history and social science" (SOL, 1995, p. i). In the foreword to the standards document, there is this statement:

> The standards are minimum requirements for each grade level, kindergarten through grade 12, in the four core subjects. The *Standards of Learning* set *reasonable targets and expectations for what teachers need to teach* [emphasis added] and students need to learn. Schools are encouraged to go beyond the prescribed standards and to enrich the curriculum to meet the needs of all students.... Parents are encouraged to work with their children to help them achieve the new academic standards (SOL, 1995, p. i).

In addition to standards for all four of the core subject areas for grade levels five and eight, there are computer and technology standards that emphasize the development of basic understanding of computer theory; basic technology skills; the processing, storing, retrieval, and transmission of electronic information; and communication through application software.

The implications of such standards and statements are far-reaching, well beyond the borders of Virginia and beyond elementary and secondary schools. These and other similar standards imply that all teachers of all disciplines must have more than these minimal skills in order to keep up with, if not to be ahead of, their own students.

The meaning is clear: Teachers at the elementary and secondary levels must receive training in technology. Most of these teachers are graduated from college or university programs that prepare them for certification or licensure. While prospective teachers are themselves students, they will receive this training from college or university faculty who, in turn, must possess those very same technology competencies.

## Research Question

With mandates for student performance being brought forward by state departments of education or public instruction, the question quickly arises: How many states require technology competencies for teachers for certification or licensure, regardless of the discipline taught? It is quite obvious that anyone teaching courses in computer science will, of necessity, have to possess a wide variety of technology competencies. For those teachers who are graduated from teacher education programs that follow the NCATE accreditation guidelines and particularly the "National Standards for Technology in Teacher Preparation," or even any modification of those guidelines and standards, those competencies are required (albeit indirectly) by the state that issues the teaching certificate, license, or endorsement.

It is not so readily obvious, however, that teachers in *all* disciplines should (1) possess such competencies, (2) possess competencies that exceed those demanded of students, (3) possess those competencies as a part of the requirements for receiving state certification or licensure for teaching. And a question that is more relevant for us as foreign language teachers is, "How can this knowledge of technology benefit my students and me?" It is clear that even though someone has a certain degree of technological acumen that person does not necessarily know how to use the knowledge effectively and efficiently.

The primary question remains: Which individual states explicitly require technology competencies for teacher certification and licensure? The information that I received from all 50 states indicated what state requirements, if any, were in place at the time of the survey (late 1999-early 2000). Respondents often mentioned requirements for teacher education programs in that state.

## Data Collection[3]

There were two primary sites that provided the essential sources of information for the survey:

(1)  "Educational Standards and Curriculum Frameworks for Technology," created and maintained by Charles Hill and the Putnam Valley (NY) Schools: On this site, Hill provides an annotated list of Internet sites with K-12 educational standards and curriculum framework documents, both by organization and by state, and including a few other countries: <http://edStandards.org/Standards.html>.

(2)  The College of Education–University of Kentucky: For this site, W. E. Stilwell and D. Hancock have attempted to collect the teacher certification requirements for the fifty states to help their students gather planning information on states in which they are interested in teaching. They point out to users of this site that states are continually revising their teacher certification or licensure rules and requirements: <http://www.uky.edu/Education/TEP/usacert.html>. For this reason, the certification and licensure information in this article must be considered the status of continually changing rules and requirements available at the time of this writing.

Using the links to offices of teacher certification and licensure provided by Stilwell and Hancock, when possible I sent a brief e-mail message to the contact person mentioned on the Web pages for that state department of education or public instruction office. If, after a reasonable period of time, I had not received a response, I contacted either the same person or another person in that office, repeating the same brief message. If there was no response, I contacted individuals outside of the office of certification or licensure.

## Analysis of Data

In late 1999 and early 2000, I sent the following original message to the offices of teacher certification or licensure:

> I have just visited your site on the Web, looking for any requirement that [*state name*] might have for technology competencies for teachers ... in all disciplines. Do you have such a requirement for your teachers? I would appreciate any help you might be able to provide.

Many responses indicated that there were technology competencies required for students in that particular state, which did not answer the original question. In cases of such a response, I again contacted the office of teacher certification or licensure and clarified the question. The types of answers that were received varied quite widely, and the amount of information that was provided was equally variable, ranging from a simple "No" in response to the research question, to the addresses of Web sites containing pertinent information, to e-mail messages from other contact persons, and finally to mailings of brochures and other information.

To simplify reporting the types of answers received, I have set up four basic categories:

(1) *Yes*: The state does explicitly require technology competencies for all teachers. The requirement appears in official state documents, rules, and regulations.

(2) *Program*: The requirement of technology competencies for all teachers is based on NCATE guidelines for the accreditation of teacher education programs. If an individual state requires that teacher education programs in colleges and universities be based on the NCATE guidelines, then the state indirectly requires technology competencies.

(3) *Indirect*: In this particular category fall those states that simply refer to "technology" in their responses to the survey or in their certification, curriculum, progress indicators, or standards. In analyzing the data, such responses were considered neither a "yes" nor a "no" answer.

(4) *No*: This group includes responses that explicitly said "no" or that did not indicate either programmatic requirements (2 above) or indirect statements (3 above). Table 1 indicates the distribution of responses to the survey question.[4]

**Table 1. Status of States with Formal Requirements for Technology Competencies for Teachers Regardless of Discipline: Distribution of Responses.**

| Yes | Program | Indirect | No |
|---|---|---|---|
| California | Alabama | Alaska | Louisiana |
| Colorado | Arkanses | Arizona | Maryland |
| Delaware | Connecticut | Hawaii | New York |
| Florida | Georgia | Maine | North Dakota |
| Idaho | Indiana | Massachusetts | Oklahoma |
| Illinois | Kansas | | Oregon |
| Iowa | Kentucky | | Rhode Island |
| Michigan | Missouri | | South Dakota |
| Minnesota | Nevada | | |
| Mississippi | New Jersey | | |
| Montana | Ohio | | |
| Nebraska | Utah | | |
| New Hampshire | Washington | | |
| New Mexico | West Virginia | | |
| North Carolina | Wisconsin | | |
| Pennsylvania | | | |
| South Carolina | | | |
| Tennessee | | | |
| Texas | | | |
| Vermont | | | |
| Virginia | | | |
| Wyoming | | | |
| N = 22 | N = 15 | N = 5 | N = 8 |

**Implications and Challenges**

As mentioned earlier, the implications of both the explicit and implicit requirements of technology competencies for teachers for certification or licensure are far-reaching, having an impact not only on PreK–12 teachers but also on postsecondary faculty members, including (and especially) those who work in teacher training programs. As ISTE (2000) points out:

> The challenge facing America's schools is the empowerment of all children to function effectively in their future, a future marked increasingly with change, information growth, and evolving technologies. Technology is a powerful tool with enormous potential

for paving high-speed highways from outdated educational systems to systems capable of providing learning opportunities for
all, to better serve the needs of 21$^{st}$ century work, communications, learning, and life (p. xi).

The goal of the NETS Project needs to and does go beyond the stated PreK-12
audience. According to the project, two of the essential conditions that must exist
to create a learning environment conducive to powerful and effective uses of technology are:

- Vision with support and proactive leadership from the education system
- *Educators skilled in the use of technology for learning* [emphasis added]
  (ISTE, 2000, p. 4).

In order for educators to become skilled in the use and integration of technology, they, just as students, must be trained. Only 8 of the 50 states (16%) have
indicated that there are currently no formal requirements for technology competencies for teachers. Of these eight, four have indicated that competencies and
standards are currently being addressed by state agencies, leaving only four that
simply answered the survey question, offering no further information. Yet, we
cannot help but believe that technology plays a major role in these four states as
well.

Learning and the development of technology skills can nonetheless take place
through individual initiative, through pre-service and in-service training programs
offered by school districts, and through professional development programs and
opportunities offered at or by colleges and universities. All school systems must
support their teachers in their efforts to create effective learning environments.
ISTE (2000, p. 4) mentions the following additional essential conditions that are
conducive to powerful uses of technology:

- Access to contemporary technologies, software, and telecommunications
  networks
- Technical assistance for maintaining and using technology resources
- Ongoing financial support for sustained technology use
- Policies and standards supporting new learning environments.

Long gone is the old saying: "Those who can, do, and those who cannot,
teach." Today it is: "Those who can, teach." And in order to teach, one must be
trained. Whether most of the teacher preparation programs adhere to NCATE or
similar standards, the learning environment for future teachers must be the same

as that for their future students, and "the most effective learning environments meld traditional approaches and new approaches to facilitate learning of relevant content while addressing individual needs," preparing students to communicate using a variety of media and formats:

- access and exchange information in a variety of ways
- compile, organize, analyze, and synthesize information
- draw conclusions and make generalizations based on information gathered
- know content and be able to locate additional information as needed
- become self-directed learners
- collaborate and cooperate in team efforts
- interact with others in ethical and appropriate ways (ISTE, 2000, p. 5).

A self-perpetuating circle exists: teacher educators train teachers who train students, some of whom will become teachers. Training in technology makes one ready for a different world. As the NETS Project (ISTE, 2000, p. 3) points out,

- **Parents want it!** Parents want their children to graduate with skills that prepare them to either get a job in today's marketplace or advance to higher levels of education and training.
- **Employers want it!** Employers want to hire employees who are honest, reliable, literate, and able to reason, communicate, make decisions, and learn.[5]
- **Communities want it!** Communities want schools to prepare their children to become good citizens and productive members of society in an increasingly technological and information-based world.
- **The nation wants it!** National leaders, the U.S. Department of Education, and other federal agencies recognize the essential role of technology in 21st century education.
- **And most of all ... kids need it!!!**

Whether an individual state explicitly requires technology competencies for all of its teachers or not, we can be sure that technology is important and that training in technology is encouraged for its teachers. We cannot ignore the vital role that technology is playing in our lives. The demand is there. It is essential that teachers, schools, school systems, and state departments of education and public instruction rise to meet the challenge. And that is just what is happening as evidenced in this survey.

**The Challenge for Foreign Language Education**

The need for and the impact of technology on teaching in general and on foreign language teaching and learning in particular should be considered from a top-down, overarching perspective–if state and school administrators do not make access to technology a priority in the state, region, or school district, no true implementation and integration of technology will filter down to the local school. In this scenario, no matter how much talk there is about the importance of technology, nothing is going to happen. Morino (2000) talks about the *digital divide*, stating that it has helped schools gain access to technology. He then asks:

> To what end? Should we not direct our energies to apply technology to improve the effectiveness of recruitment and professional development for principals and teachers? Should we not explore ways to use technology that make it easier for parents and other caring adults to become more involved with our schools? Should we not drive change that integrates technology into the curriculum and learning experience to enhance learning and improve academic achievement?

When the mandate comes from above, it must be implemented from the very top and clearly at subsequent lower levels for it to be a meaningful requirement. In certain states, the mandate for knowledge of technology comes from the state board of education and is overseen by the state office of certification or licensure. Those states believe that access to technology is necessary in their school systems and require teachers to demonstrate knowledge of technology and the ability to use it effectively. The charge is then passed down to local school districts and systems to make certain that teachers can at least maintain their current level of knowledge through additional training that the systems make available. In many states, it is the job of the educational training programs to ensure that prospective teachers are trained in technology. But just because teachers– be they in-service or pre-service teachers–must demonstrate their knowledge of technology, it follows that if they have no access to a computer at work, their knowledge cannot be kept current nor can it be put into practice.

A representative of the Hawaii department of education, acknowledging the importance of technology, has made the following statement:

> You will find several standards for which there are performance criteria that refer to technology. The Board chose not to set a standard specifically for technology because it believes it is a tool that teachers should integrate into their instruction. Creating a separate standard would have been analogous to writing a standard for using a pencil. If you read the standards and criteria

carefully, you'll also find that there are a number of places where technology can be utilized even though it is not specifically mentioned. (Mahoe, 1999)

If technology is a "tool that teachers should integrate into their instruction," then they should assuredly have immediate or relatively easy access to that technology. Access alone, however, will do no good: "We must seek purposeful use of the technology" (Morino, 2000).

What has caused this strong push toward technology? Teaching and learning are inexorably moving from the *broadcast* mode to an *interactive* mode. Broadcast technology (and, by extension, broadcast learning) is hierarchical, depending on a top-down distribution system. Television is a model for this type of technology since someone somewhere decides what will be broadcast, and our role is simply to choose to watch or not to watch. There is no direct feedback from the viewer to the broadcaster, and there is no direct interaction among viewers unless they are seated on a couch in the same room (Tapscott, 1998, p. 79).

Many teaching methods and many computer-based instruction programs are based on broadcast learning. The teacher is essentially a transmitter, relaying a curriculum designed by someone else who presumably knows best about the sequencing of material and how children learn. "Programs are not customized to each student, but rather designed to meet the needs of a grade–one-size-fits-all, like a broadcast" (Tapscott, 1998, pp. 129-30).

Interactive technology (learning), on the other hand, is exemplified by the Internet because it depends on a distributed or shared delivery system. According to Tapscott (1998) the shift from broadcast learning to interactive learning that is occurring now is taking place in eight different ways:

1. from linear, sequential/serial to hypermedia learning;
2. from instruction to construction and discovery;
3. from teacher-centered to learner-centered education;
4. from merely absorbing material to learning how to navigate and how to learn;
5. from school to lifelong learning;
6. from one-size-fits-all to customized learning;
7. from learning as torture to learning as fun;
8. from the teacher as transmitter to the teacher as facilitator (pp. 142-49).

Teachers are beginning to sense that the old broadcast view of learning is not working. The move from the position of "transmitter of knowledge" toward that of "facilitator of learning" calls for change. Tapscott (1998, p. 138) points out that "... many teachers resist change. When a shift like this occurs, leaders of the old are often the last to embrace the new. Old paradigms ... die hard. Teachers have been schooled in the broadcast mode of pedagogy." In this mode, teachers have taken new technology but continue to use it in the old mode, essentially for "drill and kill"–practice and testing.

Now we should be moving away from analog technologies that embody primarily the broadcast mode (over which we have little control) and moving toward digital technologies that encourage and facilitate interactive learning. *Analog* (broadcast) technologies include television, video, tapes, texts, books and course notes, face-to-face instruction, and overhead transparencies. *Digital* (interactive) technologies are comprised of both types of conventional computer-assisted instruction (CAI) and other types of learning environments, and the lines of demarcation of both are blurred. Examples of CAI include drills, tutorials, and games, all of which become merged into learning environments in the form of hypermedia courses, digital forums, MUDs[6] simulators, and the Word Wide Web (WWW) (Tapscott, 1998, p. 139).

The new media that we now have available have helped create a culture for learning in which the learner

> ... enjoys enhanced interactivity and connections with others. Rather than listening to some professor regurgitating facts and theories, students discuss and learn from each other with the teacher as a participant. They construct narratives that make sense out of their own experiences. Various digital forums ... enable brainstorming, debate, the influence of each other–in other words, social learning. (Tapscott, 1998, p. 141)

Now we move to the next level–the point of view of the teacher. We know that the routine use of technology, for the moment in the guise of the computer, can be limited to doing little more than facilitate teaching and record keeping: using a word processor for writing tests and creating handouts; using e-mail to stay in touch with students and parents; using the Web for easy access to authentic materials – written texts, sound clips, images; using a database or spreadsheet for recording grades. Technology, of course, goes far beyond the use of a computer; it also includes other vehicles for learning through the use of VCRs, cassette or CD players, overhead projectors, satellite dishes, and can even include the chalkboard and bulletin board. Many of these machines are available, either in the individual classroom or from the media center. Some school systems are fortunate enough to have a computer (or even more than one!) in each classroom, or at least they afford periodic access to computers in a computer laboratory.

The essential question is however: "What can the teacher do with any of this technology that will enhance learning for the students?" Indiscriminate or untrained use of technology in the classroom will not enhance learning. Having students complete homework on the Web or by e-mail is nothing more than using digital bits instead of paper and pencil to complete the very same task–a workbook by any other name remains the same. Giving students a presentation using PowerPoint, while stimulating for many faculty members, is nothing more than "just another show" from the point of view of the students. Since many of us did not grow up with PowerPoint, we find it a novel way to present information; for students who see PowerPoint presentations in almost every class, it becomes a case of what has been referred to in a Dilbert cartoon as "PowerPoint poisoning" (Adams, 2000). A poorly thought out presentation is not much more than writing on a glorified chalkboard with (often distracting) motion and occasional sounds. Using e–mail to correspond with students is not much more than handing them a note, except they can retrieve this message at home. Allowing them to write an e-mail in a foreign language without the use of appropriate accent marks, ·capitalization, and punctuation undermines what we strive for in our teaching– communicative and accurate language use.

The point is made: doing the "same old, same old" using a new manner of presentation is not an effective integration of technology into teaching. It does not enhance learning. Morino (2000) has said that "It's easy to install technology–to place a computer in a learning center–but it's difficult to change what people do in order to apply and benefit from that technology." (Technology does periodically give rise to new excuses: "My hard drive ate my homework." "My system crashed." "The line was busy and I couldn't dial in." "I lost the disk with my homework on it." "I couldn't log onto the Web because the server was down.")

> Teachers need not only a degree of facility in using any sort of technology but also a rationale for why the use of technology is better than the traditional way of presenting the material. Technology, by itself, is a thing. Silicon, wafers, and wires are amoral, neither inherently good nor inherently bad. Technology takes on importance when people apply it to a purpose. [...] ... the power of technology is not the computers, the complex of networks, or the vast databases of information. Rather it is people and their imagination, knowledge, and resourcefulness that bring about change. Technology enables people to apply their imagination and knowledge and to do so more effectively, on larger scale and, most importantly, in ways not otherwise possible." (Morino, 2000)

Technology is not to be considered an intrusion in an already overcrowded teaching schedule. It should not be considered an *in-addition-to* but an *instead-of.* Technology is not something more to be done, but something that should simplify our role as teacher, enhance the role of the student as learner, address a much wider variety of learning styles, and facilitate learning. All of these positive features of learning through technology can take place only if the teacher knows how to integrate technology into the learning process. Teachers need to know how to take advantage of what technology can offer and not simply use it as it is. This knowledge comes from training, practice, profiting from professional development opportunities (pre- and in-service workshops, training sessions, conferences, presentations), and especially from a keen desire to want to become a better, more effective teacher who stimulates students to want to learn. In "Learning Language Through Distance Education: The Challenges, Expectations, and Outcomes," Aplevich and Willment (1998, p. 64) offer a chart that will help in the selection of appropriate teaching and communication technology, depending on the medium and the particular function for which that medium is to be used. The media are divided into "courseware" (print, audio cassette, video cassette, software, CD-ROM, WWW) and "communication" (telephone tutoring, audio conferencing, video conferencing, e-mail, Internet, computer conferencing). The functions include the four skills – speaking, reading, writing, listening – culture, student to student interaction, student to instructor interaction, ease of access by student, and cost to institution.

Addressing the same most basic concern of what technology should be considered, LeLoup (1999) offers a list of basic questions that teachers should ask themselves to determine if a given communications technology will lead to optimal foreign language instruction and learning:

1.   What are my objectives for the lesson?
2.   What do I expect the students to be able to accomplish or do at the end of the lesson?
3.   Will any of these communications technologies facilitate the students' success in achieving the lesson objectives?
4.   Which, if any, communications technologies are best suited to the particular tasks I have chosen for my students to perform?
5.   Will the use of technology hinder or help the students, i.e., are they adequately and appropriately trained in the use of the technologies?
6.   Do I feel competent in using the communications technologies I am asking my students to use?
7.   Am I just using these bells and whistles because it's Friday or I didn't plan adequately for my lesson?

Once a teacher is committed to using a new technology in class, the questions and cautions arise. While there is a wealth of authentic material available for us to take into classes or to send students out to examine and study, how can we tell what material is accurate and appropriate? Textbooks are being published with a full arsenal of ancillary materials, including interactive and audio CD-ROMs, online workbooks, and Web sites. There is free-standing software available that is not connected to any particular textbook. There are Web sites throughout the world available to anyone who has access to a computer. It is worth remembering, however, that while anyone can set up a Web page, there is nothing that can vouch for the accuracy, authenticity, or appropriateness of the material included. *Caveat emptor!*

Teachers need to know how to assess the quality of materials that are available. There is much help at hand, but one must be wary of information that comes from unfamiliar sources. By using sample software reviews in the *Calico Journal,* one can devise a template for the evaluation of textbook-related and free-standing software. Rice University offers an on-line generic "Software Evaluation Guide" that raises many flags when considering the adoption or use of software: <http://www.owlnet.rice.edu/~ling417/guide.html>. Virginia Tech University also offers a similar set of generic questions to be used in evaluating Internet resources for students: <http://www.lib.vt.edu/research/evaluate/evaluating.html>. *Syllabus* magazine (August, 1999, pp. 52-54) contains an article by Hartman and Ackerman, "Finding Quality Information on the Internet: Tips and Guidelines." Specifically for the evaluation of foreign language materials–general criteria, listening, pronunciation, reading, speaking, vocabulary, and writing–there is the National Foreign Language Resource Center at the University of Hawaii at Manoa, <http://www.nflrc.hawaii.edu/aboutus/ithompson/flmedia/>. Once available materials are evaluated, selected, and purchased, how are they to be integrated into teaching in the most effective way to promote learning? As mentioned earlier, technology should not be integrated into the classroom simply for technology's sake. Technology should offer the students something different from what the teacher can offer, and yes, sometimes better than what the teacher can offer. Morino (2000) cautions,

> There is no guarantee that access to technology will produce better social outcomes like improved academic achievement .... Today too many people, afraid of being left behind in this increasingly technology-enabled world, blindly support and accept that access to technology is key to their [...] future. But that is a leap of faith.

There are many studies that have demonstrated that student performance increases when students make effective use of technology (Bush & Terry, 1997; Harper, Lively & Williams, 1998; Muyskens, 1998). The role of technology in foreign language education is also discussed in current methodology textbooks (Shrum & Glisan, 2000; Omaggio Hadley, 2001). While these sources offer much direction and guidance to the classroom teacher, they also attest to the effectiveness of technology as a means of teaching and learning, and they should be considered reference books on technology and foreign language teaching for professional libraries in all schools.

There have recently been many studies on multiple intelligences (learning styles). The use of technology can give the teacher the opportunity to address the various learning styles of students while maintaining an organized, orderly, focused classroom. If we consider the 14 different multiple intelligences that are currently being discussed, we can easily see how the integration of technology can help the teacher reach all students by appealing to their favored learning style. (See Table 2.)

**Table 2. Multiple Intelligences (Learning Styles) and Suggested Activity Types. (Haley, 2000).**

| Learning Style | Suggested Activity Types |
|---|---|
| Verbal-Linguistic | word games, storytelling, speeches, debates, jounals, dialogues, reading aloud, poetry writing, oral presentations |
| Logical-Mathematical | problem solving, math games, logic puzzles, creating codes, socratic questioning, computer programming, timelines |
| Bodily-Kinesthetic | creative movement, dance, mime, field trips, imagery, manipulatives, hands-on activities, body language, role playing |
| Visual-Spatial | diagrams, visualization, maps, visual puzzles, mind mapping, patterns, pictorial metaphors, videotaping, photography |
| Musical-Rhythmical | singing, humming, raps, chants, rhythms, listening to music, creating melodies for concepts, musical games, composing tunes |
| Naturalist | exploring outdoors, identifying flora/fauna, gardening, wildlife observation, studying natural phenomena, science projects |
| Interpersonal-Social | mediation, peer collaboration, simulations, cross-age tutoring, clubs, community projects, cooperative activities, interviews |
| Intrapersonal | individualized projects, journal writing, reflective time, quiet spaces, independent studies, self-evaluation, autobiographies |

Morino (2000) has said that the power of technology lies not in computers but rather in people and their imagination, knowledge, and resourcefulness. This, then, is the charge to teachers–establish the purpose for which the technology is planned, carefully examine what is available, evaluate it using clear criteria, integrate it into your teaching, and ... move aside. You should have chosen to use a certain technology because it offers you and your students something novel, something different, something else. It offers your students a new way to learn, a different perspective on what is being studied, and another voice. Use your imagination. Be resourceful. Determine what technology can offer your students that you cannot.

Motivating the student is of the utmost importance. Terry (1995) focuses particularly on defining motivation, how a teacher can enhance it, and just what the teacher can do. Included among his suggestions are: (1) addressing student needs and interests, (2) personalizing learning, (3) contextualizing activities, (4) choosing appropriate materials, (5) ensuring student success, and (6) recycling the elements of language. Every one of these suggestions can be facilitated through the use of technology.

If the focus is on the use of the Web in particular, one can easily understand why students can become highly motivated. They have access to the most current authentic materials:

- weather forecasts in target language countries;
- music in the target language, including the popular music for that week;
- news items with a perspective that is often quite different from the American point of view;
- an incredible variety of texts of all sorts that are available for downloading;
- synchronous and asynchronous communication virtually anywhere in the world;
- virtual tours of cities, historical sites, and monuments.

Studies have shown that normally "quiet" students who rarely participate in class activities and discussions but who use e-mail, chat rooms, MUDs (Multi-user domains), and MOOs (MUDs/object-oriented) tend to participate more readily because the idea of "performing" in front of peers is removed and a certain degree of anonymity takes charge as they assume new personae (see particularly the chapters by Kern and Beauvois in Muyskens, 1998).

Tapscott (1998) has said that new media have helped create a culture for learning, and this is where the challenge lies for teachers–all teachers. Tapscott quotes Tony Comper, President of the Bank of Montreal, who says that "Kids doing a random walk through all the information in the world is not necessarily the best way for them to learn. Teachers can become navigators providing meta-learning– crucial guidance and support regarding how to go about learning" (1998, p. 154). Professor Owston at York University in Toronto agrees: "We do have to make sure that the engagement with the Internet is stimulating and intelligent. We must remember that it's not the Internet itself that will do that–it's the teacher who mediates the student's engagement with the Internet" (cited in Tapscott, 1998, p. 154).

One local school system in Virginia instituted a program in which each secondary-level student was furnished with a laptop computer–an $18.6 million dollar investment. In an article in the local newspaper, a former business executive and a retired classroom teacher at one of that county's high schools wrote an article with the headline, "Academic Sabotage." This article is filled with cautions and with rather surprising conclusions. "Talented and challenging teachers are being systematically replaced with instructors trained in faddish technique and susceptible to superintendent policies. Now teachers no longer impart wisdom and discipline (that is, teach)–they guide students through self-instruction (facilitate)" (Wallace, 2001, p. E6).

Wallace continues: "Who's in charge? Who's really learning, and who's cutting corners with technology fake-outs" (2001, p. E6). He concludes with these statements: "Good education is dependent on good teachers–not on computers and group work.... Computers have much to offer. Yet they should be the tool, not the instructor; computers should be managed by conscientious, savvy faculty and supportive administration" (2001, p. E6).

So ... there's the challenge. There is a wealth of information available to us, most of which is now available on the Internet. We need to know how to access it. We need to know how to glean what is good and use it to its fullest advantage. We need to know how to use that information in our classes. Technology is not just for a rainy day or for when lesson plans run short. It is not something to be added into an already-crowded curriculum. It is to be used and used wisely, intelligently, effectively. It should be stimulating, motivating, and a real learning experience–an experience that affords the learner a new insight, a new perspective, a new point of view. We cannot make the learner learn. We can afford the learner every opportunity to learn. We need to guide the learner to interact with information and not just receive it from us like a broadcast.

**Notes**

[1]    The National Council for Accreditation of Teacher Education (NCATE) is the official body for accrediting teacher preparation programs, and the International Society for Technology in Education (ISTE) is the professional education organization "responsible for recommending guidelines for accreditation to NCATE for programs in educational computing and technology teacher preparation" (ISTE, 1999: <http://www.iste.org/Standards/NCATE/index.html>. At the NCATE site are the *National Standards for Technology in Teacher Preparation* recommended by the ISTE Accreditation and Standards Committee. The guidelines developed by NCATE direct those teacher preparation programs seeking accreditation to "develop a folio that addresses the performance-based standards in each matrix" (ISTE, 1999).

2    The NCATE Program Standards for Educational Computing and Technology: Educational Computing and Technology Literacy Endorsement can be found at the following Web site: <http://www.NCATE.org/standard/new%20program%20standards/iste%202001.pdf >, pp. 9-11.

3    It should be pointed out that information gleaned from Web sites is current as of the time it was originally posted (quite often the date is not indicated) and the time it was downloaded. Similarly, those Web site addresses (URLs) were fully functional at the time the information was downloaded. This does not mean that those sites still exist or that the address given is still functional.

4    The complete results of this survey can be read at the following site: <http://www.richmond.edu/~terry/Survey/start.html>.

5    In a series of Web-based and magazine articles, there has been a reaction to the fact that high-tech companies rarely hire college and university liberal arts graduates. As quoted in an article from *Time* magazine (1999, May 17), "'Our p.r. people, our marketers, even our attorneys have technical talent,' says Tracy Koon, director of corporate affairs at Intel. The need for technical expertise is so pervasive that even retailers are demanding such skills." In Virginia, the Virginia Foundation of Independent Colleges (VFIC), with input from business partners, has developed a standardized test to help students with good computing skills–but without computer-science degrees–make their expertise known to potential employers. This test, called TekXam, is an eight-part test that requires students to design a website, build and analyze spreadsheets, research problems on the Internet, and demonstrate understanding of legal and ethical issues. The creation of this test based on the career needs of liberal arts graduates begs an important question: Has the traditional liberal arts curriculum become obsolete? Mary Brown Bullock of Agnes Scott College in Atlanta says that a B.A. degree "gives graduates the ability to reinvent themselves time and time again ... and the knowledge and thinking skills that transcend a particular discipline or time frame" (cited in Kasky, 1999, p. 92).

6    According to Tapscott (1998, p. 174), "A MUD is a 'place' on the Net where users create their own dramatic adventures in real-time. Other forms of MUDs are MUSEs, MOOs, and MUSHs, depending on the software tools used in constructing the experience. [...] MUDs, or Multi User Dungeons (also called multi user dimensions), were initially text-based virtual realities. Unlike chat room exchanges, MUDs host intensive, ongoing games in which online characters are constructed over months and adventures are played out over weeks."

## References

Adams, Scott. (2001, August 16). *Dilbert* [Cartoon].

Bush, M. D. & Terry, R. M. (Eds.). (1997). *Technology-enhanced language learning.* The ACTFL Foreign Language Education Series. Lincolnwood, IL: National Textbook Company.

Haley, M. H. (2000). *Multiple intelligences research study* [On-line]. Available: <http://gse.gmu.edu/research/mirs>.

Harper, J., Lively, M. G., & Williams, M. K. (1998). *The coming of age of the profession: Issues and emerging ideas for the teaching of foreign languages.* Boston: Heinle & Heinle Publishers.

Hartman, K., & Ackerman, E. (1999). Finding quality information on the Internet: Tips and guidelines. *Syllabus, 13* (1), 52-54.

Hill, C. (1999). *Educational standards and curriculum frameworks for technology.* Putnam Valley (NY) Schools [On-line]. Available: <http://edStandards.org/Standards.html>.

International Society for Technology in Education. (1999). *National standards for technology in teacher preparation* [On-line]. Available: <http://www.iste.org/standards/ncate/index.html>.

International Society for Technology in Education. (2000). *National educational technology standards for students: Connecting curriculum and technology.* Eugene, OR: author.

Kasky, J. (1999, May 17). Wanted: Well-read techies. *Time, 92.*

LeLoup, J. *Targeting pedagogy* [On-line]. Available: <http://www.cortland.edu/flteach/methods/obj3/intro3.html>.

Mahoe, S. C. (1999). Hawaii Teacher Standards Board. Personal communication.

Morino, M. (2000, October 30). *Policy and philanthropy: Keys to closing the digital divide.* Remarks at Networks for People 2000 Conference [On-line]. Available: <http://morino.org/closing_sp_dig.asp>.

Muyskens, J. A., ed. (1998). *New ways of learning and teaching: Focus on technology and foreign language education.* AAUSC Issues in Language Program Direction. Boston: Heinle & Heinle Publishers.

North Carolina Department of Public Instruction. (1999). NC Technology competencies for educators [On-line]. Available: <http://www.dpi.state.nc.us/tap/techcomp.htm>.

North Carolina Department of Public Instruction–Office of Financial and Personnel Services. (1999) [On-line]. Available: <http://www.dpi.state.nc.us/tap/basic.htm> and <http://www.dpi.state.nc.us/tap/basic.htm>.

Omaggio Hadley, A. (2001). *Teaching language in context* (3rd ed.). Boston: Heine & Heinle Publishers.

Rice University. (n.d.). Software evaluation guide [On-line]. Available: <http://www.owlnet.rice.edu/~ling417/guide.html>.

Shrum, J. L. & Glisan, E. W. (2000). *Teacher's handbook: Contextualized language instruction* (2nd ed.). Boston: Heinle & Heinle Publishers.

*Standards of learning for Virginia public schools.* (1995). Richmond, VA: Commonwealth of Virginia, Board of Education.

Stilwell, W.E., & Hancock, D. (1999). *50 states' certification requirements.* Lexington, KY: The College of Education [On-line]. Available: <http://www.uky.edu/Education/TEP/usacert.html>.

Tapscott, D. (1998). *Growing up digital: The Rise of the net generation.* New York: McGraw-Hill.

Terry, R. M. (1995). Pragmatic reflections on motivation in the L2 classroom. In G. K. Crouse (Ed.), *Broadening the frontiers of foreign language education* (pp. 1-18) Report of the Central States Conference on the Teaching of Foreign Languages. Lincolnwood, IL: National Textbook Company.

Virginia Tech University. (n.d.). *Evaluating web information* [On-line]. Available: <http://www.lib.vt.edu/research/evaluate/evaluating.html>

Wallace, R. (2001, November 11). Student computers have upstaged Henrico teachers. *Richmond Times-Dispatch,* p. E6.

# 2
# K-6 Spanish by Distance Laerning: Media Pedagogy as an Effective Resource for the Classroom Teacher

Zoe Louton
Nebraska State Department of Education

## Introduction

This article reports the interim findings of an exploratory component of IN-VISION, a federally funded technology project in Iowa and Nebraska. Our project addresses three primary questions: (1) How effective are distance learning technologies as instructional tools for the young learner? (2) What new pedagogical approaches are required when the teacher and students are not in the same physical location? (3) How can distance learning technologies enrich and extend the curriculum while enhancing the role of the classroom teacher? With educational reform as a guiding principle in the grant specifications, our program staff has sought various ways to provide access to Spanish language-learning opportunities for students in rural and disadvantaged elementary schools, students who would otherwise have little or no contact with a foreign language and its culture.

Secondary schools, faced with a critical shortage of qualified teachers, have opted in a few cases for Web-based courses, but many schools in the Midwest have chosen distance learning systems. Therefore, distance learning rooms have become a commonplace fixture in secondary schools and distance learning courses are firmly established in curricular offerings. This expansion has taken place in spite of the all-too-frequent lack of preparation, planning, and understanding of effective distance learning strategies on the part of the teacher or facilitator (Curtain & Pesola, 1994).

Most elementary students, however, have no access to distance learning. Some states, having mandated elementary foreign language instruction, have chosen videotaped courses to be shown by the classroom teacher, with limited opportunities for student practice and interaction. Thus, for most elementary students, foreign language learning opportunities remain limited to the capacities of the local school.

Our staff, nevertheless, wanted to learn whether elementary students, given distance learning opportunities, would relate positively not only to the foreign language, but also to the new medium. Would they feel detached from the presentation and interaction with the distant instructor, or would they develop and maintain attention, motivation, and an appropriate learning set? We wanted to find a distance learning approach that would engage the young learners and involve them in the Spanish sessions. Equally important, we wanted the classroom teacher to remain an integral and essential part of the process.

### Distance Learning Overview

Distance learning has assumed an ever-increasing presence in the field of education, creating the need for a new dimension in pedagogy that uses various technologies to mediate the distance between the learner and the learning resource. These emerging technologies and the evolving learner-centered educational philosophy provide the means and the social framework for a new pedagogy.

In the traditional face-to-face classroom pedagogy, the teacher (as the link between the learner and the learning resources) is the perceived manipulator of the educational process. Distance learning, however, links the learner *directly* to the resources by means of various technological tools, with the instructor either unseen (as in on-line learning) or physically absent (as in desktop conferencing or in a distance learning room). This places the learner in a constructivist position as the manipulator seeking to connect with the material, with the medium now as deliverer of the message. The instructor's presence decreases, but his or her role is optimized in increased preparation, organization, presentation, and attentiveness to the learning process. The instructor is now truly a facilitator who:

- Sets the stage with rich materials that promise access to even more rewarding resources.
- Devises engaging ways to present the material to learners.
- Initiates strategies to accommodate the learner from a distance and to develop materials that encourage further engagement.
- Finds ways to interact with the learners from an offstage position, maintaining the impetus for interaction that comes from the learner, not the facilitator.
- Finds ways to achieve rapid feedback and assess progress remotely in order that the process be effective.

This is a radical change from the practice of merely transplanting a course from the traditional classroom to a media setting. This latter practice, all too common, invites learner dissatisfaction and eventual disillusionment with media learning (Wilson, 2001).

Yet, the demand for distance learning at the secondary, collegiate, and adult levels is constantly outpacing the supply of organized virtual learning opportunities. Virtual universities around the world as well as real universities offer a wide range of courses and full degree programs for participants (Bok, 1990; Dertouzos, 1997). One sees in this movement the beginnings of a new media-centered pedagogical approach manifested in the increasing number of offerings in distributive education, as well as in the requests for new personnel as instructional designers in distributive education.

What about the younger learner, however? Distance learning has centered mainly on older students: high school, university, and adult. The belief has been that both self-discipline and motivation are essential to maintain learner interest and attention in the absence of personal oversight such as that provided by the teacher in the traditional classroom. Thus, distance learning at the elementary level is largely an under-explored field. The demand for it rarely surfaces, even though the children's needs mirror those of the older students: geographical isolation (both rural and urban), budgetary constraints, and teacher shortage. Children do not demonstrate the characteristics usually considered essential for distance learning, especially that of self-discipline. One must ask if there are elements in the child's approach to learning that would minimize the "distance effect" that many older learners have to overcome.

## Project Evolvement

Our grant project was initiated in 1997 with eight participating elementary schools in Nebraska and Iowa. One initial project goal was to develop and implement effective strategies for media learning at the elementary level in order to address the increasing need for supplementary learning opportunities, particularly for those in disadvantaged circumstances. Foreign language (Spanish) was selected as the experimental subject matter for two primary reasons. First, being usually excluded from the general education curriculum of elementary teacher preparation, foreign language is least accessible for most elementary students. Second, learning a foreign language requires a wealth of interaction and has been considered less amenable to distance education. Thus, our hypothesis was that if elementary students can learn foreign language successfully by distance means, the process might be applicable to other elementary subject areas as well. The basic initial design included:

- An instructional video in Spanish that the students viewed once or twice a week.
- Suggested activities for the implementation of the video lesson that the classroom teacher could integrate with other daily classroom activities.
- Twice-a-month staff development sessions for the classroom teachers in their local distance learning rooms.
- Technology-training opportunities for the teachers, exposing them to supplementary Web, Internet, and software resources.
- On-site visits to the classrooms once or twice a week by paraprofessionals to provide language modeling and practice.

The first-year evaluation reported that the students and teachers were indeed learning Spanish effectively by this design. The evaluation team from the National K-12 Foreign Language Resource Center at Iowa State University assessed the students based on the expanded version of the rating scale for the Student Oral Proficiency Assessment (SOPA). Most (95.2%) were found to be at the Junior Novice Mid level for *comprehension*. As is usual for beginning students, language *production* lagged as 99% were rated at the Junior Novice Low level for fluency (Rosenbusch, 1999, p. 17). While the teachers were not the primary focus of language instruction, they themselves achieved the equivalent of a Novice Low/Novice Mid rating as measured by the Self-Assessment of Spanish Speaking Skills instrument developed by the Center for Applied Linguistics (p. 14).

It was believed that the lack of a specialist teacher was compensated for in part by students' weekly contact with the paraprofessional. But perhaps equally important was the students' realization that their teacher was learning along with them and was encouraging use of Spanish throughout the school day and in contexts other than the Spanish lesson.

In its first year, foreign language instruction proved to be popular with the students and teachers. They appreciated the availability of this resource as a connection to the larger world. The teachers were generally comfortable with their language abilities. One teacher wrote:

> It has been fun and exciting for my students as well as for me. I don't look upon myself as a teacher of Spanish as I am definitely a learner myself. I view myself as a facilitator–using the great materials provided to facilitate the children's learning of Spanish (Rosenbusch, 1999, p. 13).

### Distance Learning Rooms

We recognized that even though a language specialist guided the curriculum from a distance, the paraprofessional was the *de facto* on-site "teacher" by modeling pronunciation, providing language practice, and encouraging interaction. While this is not yet a "true" distance learning design, the basic framework was set to move toward a more authentic distant instruction by having the paraprofessional "visit" solely via distance learning technology. The original instructional design would continue even as the number of participants would increase to include 16 schools.

During the second year, we scheduled three weekly sessions of 20 minutes each with two second-grade classrooms in the distance learning room at their school (the remote site) and the paraprofessional in another town (the host site). In planning the sessions, we concentrated on three questions: (1) Will the students' attention remain focused on the monitors? (2) Will students interact comfortably with the instructor seen only on the monitor? (3) Can the students effectively learn new material this way?

We had to overcome the disadvantages presented by the rooms themselves, which are set up mainly for older students. The size of the chairs and tables, the lecture room arrangement, and the requirement that the elementary student must concentrate on monitors well above eye level, all exclude the establishment of a suitable learning environment for small children. In order to facilitate comfort and ease of movement, we pushed tables and chairs to the side and permitted children at the remote site to sit on the floor. A simple garden backdrop and stuffed animal props at the host site served as a stimulus for imagination and fantasy. With the classroom teacher facilitating as the on-site member of the instructional team, the environment became an extension of the classroom.

The paraprofessional made extensive use of communication-based strategies for maximum student involvement: games and stories for motivation and meaningful language practice (Egan, 1986) and manipulatives on the overhead document camera to aid comprehension and interest. The first two sessions each week reviewed material covered previously in the classroom sessions, while the third session introduced new material. Throughout the sessions, students focused directly on the activities and materials on the monitor as if there were no distance between them and the instructor. They demonstrated comprehension by responding unhesitatingly when requested, using Spanish almost unconsciously (i.e., they focused more on the content of the instruction than on the language). The student responses during the session plus the language acquisition they demonstrated subsequently in the classroom (as reported by the paraprofessional and the classroom teacher) indicated that the students were able to learn effectively in a distance setting. We felt that we had a significant positive reaction to the initial three questions that drove our experiment.

During the 2000-01 school year, we continued with four trial distance learning sessions, inviting participation from three schools that use combined K-12 buildings with easy access to the distance learning rooms. These sessions would supplement, not replace, any scheduled on-site visit by the paraprofessional. Eight teachers volunteered to participate, with grade levels ranging from kindergarten through sixth grade. To allow for more direct contact with the images on the monitor, we connected a projector to the console, displaying the images onto the wall. This presented the images in large format, permitted eye-level viewing, and gave easy assess for physical contact with images displayed there (e.g., students were able to touch parts of images projected onto the wall when they were requested to do so).

The lesson content utilized general vocabulary already familiar to the children while introducing new words and cultural topics. As during the previous year, contextualized teaching strategies and activities were designed to engage the students' interest and invite interactivity: guessing games, songs, dances, and stories. A new feature introduced was interactive programs from the host-site computer that were displayed on the wall for the students at the remote site, providing further contexts where the students needed the language to participate. As the students touched images on the wall, the instructor at the host site clicked on the corresponding items on her computer, providing, as Asher (1986) advocated, a tactical link with the language. For example, the teacher would command, "Point to the horse." As the student complied, there was the sound of approval from the computer (i.e., immediate reinforcement). Then followed a subsequent request in the form of task-based instruction (Lee, 1995), "Put the horse in the barn." The student touched the horse image, which then moved *onto* the barn. The simultaneous click on the computer at the host site put the horse *into* the barn. The students' attention focused on the perceived effect of the hand movement, not on the instructor or the Spanish prompt. This showed that learner engagement with the learning process appeared to be more essential than the physical presence of the instructor. Meanwhile, the instructor monitored the student responses for pacing and comprehension. The result was judged to be successful in terms of student responses and achievement of learning goals. Students maintained direct contact with the learning source, interacted enthusiastically, and learned the new material effectively, enabling them to use the new vocabulary and concepts in subsequent sessions.

### On-line Instruction

In this the third year (2001-2002), we continue further implementation of a media-based pedagogy. In addition to continuing the two-way audiovisual format for those classes with distance learning room access, we are exploring the effectiveness of an on-line format for others with no such access, in this case, three fourth-grade classes in one school. A content-based approach works particularly well here because, with the relative invisibility of the Spanish instructor, the content becomes not only a meaningful vehicle for the language but a virtual extension of the classroom teacher and curriculum.

The content focus is a year-long study of five regions of the United States. The unit design for each region involves asynchronous instruction by interactive CDs and synchronous instruction by desktop conferencing sessions using NetMeeting. This overall design accommodates a variety of learning preferences. Each unit proceeds as follows:

1.  The unit begins with CD #1, which presents vocabulary and pronunciation, using visuals and interactive strategies as it reviews the material already covered in English by the classroom teacher. Students work at the classroom computers, either individually, in pairs, or in groups of three. Copies of the CD may be taken home for further practice.

2.  The first desktop conference with the Spanish specialist is then conducted to expand the language practice and reinforce the subject matter. This is implemented in various ways to accommodate the objectives of the classroom teacher. A few students at a time can arrange themselves in front of

the computer camera; or, with the use of a projector, the image can be displayed in large format. The classroom teacher facilitates the students' interaction with the camera and with each other. The session can also be taped for further practice and used either individually or in groups.

3.  The unit continues with CD #2, which presents a wealth of mostly interactive situations for language practice from which the student can choose. Activities include playing *Hangman*, using flashcards, performing matching exercises, completing short answer questions, solving jigsaw puzzles, answering multiple choice questions, playing *Jeopardy,* unscrambling sentences, identifying pictures, and playing *Who Wants to Be a Millionaire?* There is also a selection of Internet links for further resources and virtual field trips. At the discretion of the teacher, students may choose to create a simple multimedia presentation to share with the other classes.

4.  The unit concludes with the students' second desktop Spanish session, permitting further real-time language practice and evaluation.

## Observations

Our experiences have revealed in the young learner unexpected potential for media-based learning. Perhaps this format resembles children's television programs sufficiently that we are actually tapping into a process already familiar to the students. In order to be economically viable, successful television shows for children must accommodate the child's unique learning style. Such programs include a variety of rich visual and sound clips that depict developmentally appropriate messages. The child can connect with these messages and invest them with meaning. Children have no difficulty identifying with the message or responding to and even interacting with the characters on the screen.

The responses of young children to the distance learning session seem to become an extension of their accustomed responses to children's television programs. For these learners, there is no "remote" effect often experienced by secondary students that makes attending to the distance learning session difficult, resulting in a detachment from the learning process. Instead, in our sessions we observed the young learners making an apparent "direct connection" with the remote learning source. Reality was suspended as they spontaneously spoke and interacted with the monitors and the images projected onto the wall. The virtual session easily became their reality for that short time. A six-year-old boy showed just how strong this effect can be. When the system was turned off at the end of the session, he blinked his eyes, ran up to the wall and, touching it, said in a wondering voice, "It's a *wall!*" The young students' immersion in the distance learning program reflects a similar focus when these same students watch *Sesame Street* or *Mr. Rogers.* The children frequently respond verbally to these television programs, learning and practicing new words and concepts. Likewise, attention span is not a problem for young students in the distance learning classroom, and the concentrated time on-task produces a rich learning experience.

In some ways, distance learning strategies resemble a similar presentation technique used in face-to-face sessions. Teachers who use children's books in the foreign language classroom are taking advantage of the language learning process inherent in children. The environment is safe and familiar, and the books provide a language immersion directed by a wealth of visuals that reflect the message (Moeller, 1999). The students focus on the meaning communicated by the pictures, support it with the words they know, and acquire new vocabulary as the teacher demonstrates meaning during the reading. Likewise, in distance learning, the monitor serves as an analogue to children's books. If the session is properly prepared with a rich and varied selection of visuals and strategies for understanding that involve the students, they will listen, respond, and interact with the image projected, either spontaneously or as requested.

Media-based learning requires a pedagogical approach that begins with the physical absence of the course instructor, and so it is ideally suited to a constructivist approach. In fact, if the theoretical approach is not learner-centered, there is little hope for meaningful student interaction with the remote learning source. Just as in choosing to interact with Mr. Rogers, students in a distance learning session must perceive *themselves* as making the direct connection with the learning source, with no one else directing each step. Links for choices are offered in on-line activities, but the students make their own selections. This has important implications for foreign language learning.

In learning a second language, as in learning their own language, children are immersed in words while focusing on understanding the message. When their attention is riveted on a message *they* want to understand, children use the words they know, acquire a few new ones that seem to fit the message, and intuit the rest. This intuition creates a direct connection with the message, allowing them to divine meaning that is satisfactory for them because it is *their* meaning. However, when the pressure for understanding comes from *outside* themselves, their entire focus changes to cope with the requestor rather than the message to be understood.

The instructional design of distance learning lessons must incorporate a wealth of educational activities and products that reflect an awareness of learning preferences and the requirements of a distance learning format. The minimal basic precepts for successful learning are: (1) avoidance of excessive information presented at any one time since this causes distraction and a loss of information just acquired; (2) reinforcement of new material through repetition and presentation of quantities of amplifying material; and (3) use of multiple methods of information presentation.

With the monitor or screen as the focal point for the delivery of information, the audio-visual impact of a lesson becomes a primary consideration, especially when studies show that after ten days students remember 10% of what they have read, 20% of what they have heard, and 30% of what they have seen and heard.

Although we acquire information through all our senses, about 75% comes from sight, 13% through hearing, only 6% through touch, and 3% shared by taste and smell (Parker et. al., 1997). With such a large proportion of information gained through sight, visual stimulation is important, especially for the young learner who has not yet gained a strong dependence on words.

Listening is also important. The average person speaks at the rate of 125 to 150 words per minute, but the brain can process words at speeds of 300 words or more per minute (Parker et al., 1997). It might be that the young learner, not knowing all the words, uses this time for intuiting meaning, based on the available contextual clues. Visualization of ideas and concepts, often optional in the face-to-face classroom, becomes important for children in media learning which, with the monitor or screen, becomes a visual medium (Cyrs, 1997). Just as television graphics in children's shows capitalize on skills that invite "visual thinking" and are ideally suited to the young mind, so should media learning include the construction of word pictures, visual analogy, magic allusion, hand-drawn figures, and the ability to visualize a story.

The classroom teacher is the ideal facilitator for media-based learning, whether it occurs on-line or in the distance learning room. The teacher prepares the class for the media session by communicating its relationship to the curriculum, then facilitating as needed during the session, and extending the lesson after the session to tie it to the developing classroom concepts. For the student, the familiar presence of the classroom teacher helps establish the learning environment and promote the learning process. For the classroom teacher, distance learning technologies provide access to an infinite array of information, materials, tools, and specialists to support the curriculum, while enriching learning opportunities in the classroom. The teacher is freed from the responsibility of having to be the total repository of information for the students and can instead better guide them toward developing their own learning goals and skills.

Because of the results of the past three years, we look forward to additional insights into media learning for children as newer distance technologies develop. Today much distance learning courseware is technically primitive because it uses older Internet technology, such as Listserv news or discussion groups (text-based), low-end e-mail systems, low bandwidth Internet connections that do not adequately support simultaneous audio/video communication, and text-based Web pages (also without audio, video, or interactivity). With the exception of some e-mail "keypal" activities, these applications have not been sufficiently adaptable to children's distance learning. Fortunately, delivery systems are improving.

Using software such as NetMeeting, instructors are holding desktop video-conferencing to talk to older students in groups or one-on-one, whether students are located at home or in the classroom. Because NetMeeting supports interactivity, it is being used widely for foreign language teaching in the rapidly growing home schooling market. We find it works very well for our on-line, real-time sessions; the children interact with it as easily as they do with the other monitors, especially when it is projected on the wall in large format.

We anticipate including newer technological developments such as voice chat rather than text. Voice chat facilitates oral communication in a foreign language and does not require typing skills of the younger children. The software, such as PalTalk, supports several participants at a time discussing whatever is on the screen, with the course instructor assisting in the orderliness of the discussion from a distance, just as the teacher in a face-to-face classroom would do.

Another new system appearing in schools in Nebraska and Iowa is PowerPlay, a portable distance learning room on a cart that rolls into individual classrooms. It supports seven remote sites simultaneously with the host distance instructor, and it has all the same technology available in a distance learning room. The advantage for children is that the environment is familiar, and the classroom teacher can enhance and implement the distance session with classroom material and activities. Of course, we will again project the monitor image on the wall to make it more accessible to the children.

As the developing technologies become available for media-based learning, we eagerly look forward to the accompanying development of a new vision of learning environments, content, and pedagogy that is appropriate to distance learning. This will provide a much-increased variety of resources to the classroom teacher, as well as an increased access to learning opportunities for elementary students. The exciting reward is in the success and enthusiasm shown by the students themselves, who are so amenable to media-based learning.

## References

Asher, J. J. (1986*). Learning another language through actions: The complete teacher's guidebook* (3rd ed.). Los Gatos, CA: Sky Oaks Publications.

Bok, D. (1990). *Universities and the future of America.* Durham, NC: Duke University Press.

Curtain, H. & Pesola, C. A. (1994). *Languages and children: Making the match.* New York: Longman.

Cyrs, T. E. & Conway, E. D. (1997). *Teaching at a distance with the merging technologies: An instructional systems approach.* Las Cruces, NM: New Mexico State University Center for Educational Development.

Dertouzos, M. (1997). *What will be: How the new world of information will change our lives.* San Francisco: HarperCollins.

Egan, K. (1986). *Teaching as storytelling.* Chicago: The University of Chicago Press.

Lee, J. (1995). Using task-based instruction to restructure class discussions. *Foreign Language Annals, 28*, 437-446.

Moeller, A. J. & Meyer, R. J. (1995). Children's books in the foreign language classroom: Acquiring natural language in familiar contexts. In G. K. Crouse (Ed.), *Broadening the frontiers of foreign language education* (pp. 33-45). Report of the Central States Conference on the Teaching of Foreign Languages. Lincolnwood, IL: National Textbook Company.

Parker, L., Parker, A. & Hough, J. (1997). *Making connections: Tips, tactics and strategies that work for distance educators*. Stillwater, OK: Parker Consulting Teletraining Institute.

Rosenbush, M., Padgitt, J. & Garcia, E. (1999). IN-VISION technology challenge grant, annual evaluation report [On-line]. Available: <http://www.educ.iastate.edu/nflrc/invision>.

Wilson, D. (2001, August 30). Educational disconnect in online learning. Los Angeles *Times* [On-line]. Available: <http://www.latimes.com/news/education/la-000070112aug30.column?coll=la-news-learning>.

**Suggested Readings**

Berge, Z. & Collins, M. (1995). Computer-mediated communication and the online classroom in distance learning. *Computer-mediated communications magazine* [On-line], 2. Available: <http://sunsite.unc.edu/cmc/mag/1995/apr/berge.html>.

Blackmore, J. (1996). *Pedagogy: Learning styles* [On-line]. Available: <http://granite.cyg.net/~jblackmo/diglib/styl-a.html>.

Diaz, D. P. & Botenbal, K. F. (2000). Pedagogy-based technology training. In P. Hoffman & D. Lemke (Eds.), *Teaching and learning in a network world* (pp. 50-54). Amsterdam, Netherlands: IOS Press.

Duffy, T. M. & Cunningham, D. J. (1998). Constructivism: Implications for the design and delivery of instruction. In D. J. Jonassen (Ed.), *Handbook of research for educational communications and technology* (pp. 170-198). New York: Simon & Schuster Macmillan.

Miller, S. M., & Miller, K. L. (1999). Using instructional theory to facilitate communication in Web-based courses. *Educational Technology & Society, 2*, 106-114.

Piaget, J. (1963). *The language and thought of the child*. New York: W. W. Norton.

Schuyler. G. (1997). A paradigm shift from instruction to learning. *ERIC Digests* [Online]. Available: <http://www.gseis.ucla.edu/ERIC/digests/dig9802.html>.

# 3

# Francophone Cultures and the Web: An Integrated, Standards-Based Approach to Teaching Culture

**Jayne Abrate**
AATF, Southern Illinois University

It is widely accepted that knowledge of the target culture is essential to successful communication in the target language, that culture is "...part of the process of living and being in the world, the part that is necessary for making meaning" (Robinson-Stuart & Nocon, 1996, p. 432). Learners must know of the interdependence of culture and language in order to advance beyond the expression of basic needs to meaningful communication on a variety of topics. Similarly, they must progress beyond learning mere facts about a culture toward a more thorough understanding and appreciation. Textbooks, by their nature, can present only static, anecdotal, and rapidly outdated glimpses of other cultures. It is the responsibility of the teacher to supplement these presentations with materials and experiences that allow students to develop the skills to observe and analyze cultural phenomena on their own. A year-long, content-based project organized around Francophone cuisines and the use of Internet resources provides opportunities for students to practice communication and cultural observation and to develop a greater understanding of the target culture.

A long-term project facilitates the internalization of open-minded cultural observations as well as the integration of language skills within a context. Lee (1997) notes that "...by using Internet tools for developing students' C2 knowledge and awareness, students can begin to explore both language and culture in a meaningful context" (p. 421). The Internet opens the door to an endless supply of authentic documents in French, thus offering students a direct view of cultural products and practices. Additionally, Internet resources permit the teacher to broaden the cultural focus from France to the entire French-speaking world with a wealth of information that would be otherwise unavailable. In fact, "...the WWW must be considered the single best source for authentic documents" (Walz, 1998, p. 104). The theme of Francophone cuisine provides a rich cultural environment that can be explored over many weeks, highlighting diverse regions of the Francophone world, addressing all the national standards, and leading students beyond typical stereotypes into a more in-depth analysis of cultural perspectives.

The interrelatedness of language and culture and the use of the target language in and out of the classroom pervade the *Standards for Foreign Language Learning in the 21st Century* (National Standards in Foreign Language Education Project, 1999) and are illustrated graphically by its "weave of curricular elements" (p. 33). Walz (1998) asserts: "One can say that the Standards make content-based education the norm and that content is the daily-life culture of the people who speak the target language" (p. 104). The Standards document presents brief scenarios to demonstrate how teachers have incorporated multiple standards into classroom activities. However, projects that are larger in scope permit the inclusion over time of all the *Standards'* five Cs: *Communication, Cultures,* and *Comparisons*, which are the goals most easily addressed on a daily basis; *Connections* and *Communities*, which require more forethought.

The three modes of *communication* are intertwined throughout this content-based project. An interesting cultural theme like cuisine encourages and motivates students to communicate early, and their work with authentic documents shows them how they can use their nascent language skills for a real purpose. Interpersonal communication occurs during small group work but may also take place with correspondents via e-mail or with outside cultural informants. Students can interpret authentic documents or analyze the presentations of guest lecturers. Presentational communication is incorporated in the form of oral or written assignments and reports, posters, demonstrations, Web pages, or PowerPoint presentations. Since it is important to maintain the use of French insofar as possible during the activities, the use of Internet technology should remain subordinate to the linguistic and cultural content.

Cuisine and the habits related to it offer many examples of products and practices of French-speaking *cultures*. The perspectives that underlie them can often be observed and discussed, although support from the teacher or from outside cultural informants may prove helpful. *Comparisons* arise naturally from the familiar subject matter and the students' initial application of the learners' own cultural lens to the target culture. The teacher's role must be to refocus that lens so that it observes cultural phenomena in their own context. Students can then learn not to make judgements based on their own underlying assumptions regarding culture. Linguistic comparisons also occur naturally and can be encouraged by the teacher.

*Connections* in the form of interdisciplinary links through guest lectures, support from fellow teachers of other subjects, or student research constitute part of the project. Students research the Francophone cuisine theme on their own via the Internet and use technology to learn about other subjects. If the project includes participation by target-language speakers from the community or correspondence with native speakers via e-mail, students are able to use the context of cuisine to participate in the larger world *community*.

Eating habits and traditions are among the most pervasive and most subconscious elements of culture. Food is associated not only with daily life but with family relationships, social interaction, economics, and religion. Nearly everyone who experiences a new culture for the first time has immediate and sometimes overpowering reactions to food. American students often have very definite likes and dislikes when it comes to eating. Consequently, a food-related project provides students with a context for cultural observation that is both familiar and fraught with stereotypical responses.

The use of French and Francophone cuisines as an organizer for this project offers itself readily to multiple levels of interpretation. Activities can easily be spiraled to more difficult linguistic and cognitive levels as students progress. Language skills and concepts can be reinforced and expanded. English can be used, when necessary, to allow students to discuss important cultural phenomena, but most tasks and activities can be conducted in French. The topic can also be expanded to include other disciplines (e.g., geography, history, nutrition, social studies, art, music, or political science). Finally, students become "...responsible for researching and synthesizing information on cultural topics. Then we may build on their research to create communicative activities to facilitate language practice and design activities to promote critical thinking and understanding" (Jourdain, 1998, p. 441). As the project develops, students can gain more autonomy in managing the activities and may, in fact, compete among themselves to contribute to its success.

## Description of Project [1]

The Francophone cuisine project described here is intended for third- or fourth-year high school students or third- or fourth-semester university students. In-class activities are designed for groups of four who spend about 30 minutes per week of class time on the project. It is assumed that students have Internet access outside of class and that someone in each group has some familiarity with Internet searches and Web pages. Targeted standards are listed with the assignments in the same format used in the Standards document.

### *Overall Assignment*

You are going to organize and participate in a Francophone cooking contest toward the end of the school year. School officials and others will be invited to serve as judges. The class will also produce an illustrated Francophone cookbook. The class will be divided into groups of four, and each group will choose a region of France and four Francophone countries, select typical recipes from each area, select a menu that includes one dish (appetizer, soup, main course, vegetable, dessert) from each geographic area, and prepare one of these recipes for the contest. The cookbook should contain the best recipes, information about their place of origin, and illustrations.

**Proposed Schedule**

### *Weeks 1-2: Summary*

In launching a content-based project, Turnbull (1999) advises that "...the beginning step of any unit is designed to allow students and teachers to pool their preexisting knowledge (linguistic and content) of the topic area..." (p. 550). Building on the students' prior exposure to French cuisine, the teacher gives an overview of French and Francophone cuisines, meal composition and courses, nutrition, and climactic and geographic influences on food production and consumption. A limited introduction to these topics will suffice as preparation for the activities to follow, but this presentation can be expanded and parallel activities incorporated with the help of teachers from other disciplines or guest speakers. This introduction also provides an opportunity to begin examining the students' cultural biases and common stereotypes as they pertain to food and eating. If necessary, some introduction to Internet resources, search engines, and saving and printing files and images can be added.

### *Week 3*

The teacher divides the class into groups of four, ensuring that each group has at least one member with Internet experience. Each group chooses a region of France. The teacher can distribute a handout containing basic vocabulary and expressions. However, rather than simply giving a list of terms, new items can be presented in questionnaire form. This questionnaire can begin with simple yes-no questions so that students can practice manipulating the new vocabulary and proceed to more complex questions: *Is the recipe easy or difficult to prepare? Are the ingredients expensive? What is the most expensive ingredient? Are the ingredients and utensils easily available? How much time is needed to prepare this recipe? Would you like to eat this dish? Why or why not?* This questionnaire not only provides students with appropriate vocabulary but guides their consideration of content.

*Assignment*

Using the list given by your teacher, locate the regions of France on a map and select one for further investigation. With a partner from your group, using a French search engine,[2] look for recipes from your region, with images if possible. Try to find at least six recipes from different course categories—appetizer, soup, main course, vegetable, dessert. Save the recipes and images on a diskette and print a copy.

In your group during class time, create a master list organized by course that includes the recipes found by each pair. Using the questionnaire given, sort the recipes by feasibility (e.g., time and equipment needed, cost, availability of ingredients), although you do not need to devote a great deal of time to understanding the complete text of the recipes.

*Targeted Standards and Reflection*

1.1 **Interpersonal Communication**: Students work in groups to organize a list of dishes.
1.2 **Interpretive Communication**: Students read and interpret recipes in French.
2.2 **Products of Culture**: Students learn about various French dishes and foods.
3.1 **Making Connections**: Students increase their knowledge of French food and cooking.
3.2 **Acquiring Information**: Students use the Internet to find recipes in French.

The teacher collects the master lists and verifies that the recipes are correctly organized, noting any feasibility problems. Copies should then be made for each member of the group and for the teacher.

## Week 4

On the Internet, students locate and organize cultural and geographic information about their region. The teacher prepares a master form on which students enter the information they have gathered.

*Assignment*

With a partner, perform an Internet search on your region looking for geographic and cultural information. One pair from each group looks for geographic information: (1) the names of the *départements* that comprise the region with the (2) *chef-lieu* (chief town) of each, (3) the region's topology, (4) the population, (5) the largest city, and images including (6) a map and (7) a picture of the largest city. The second pair looks for cultural information: (1-2) two historical facts, (3-4) two famous people native to the region, (5) an agricultural or food product for which the region is known, and images including (6-7) two monuments and (8) one of the famous people. Save the information and images on a diskette and print a copy.

In your group during class time, create a master portrait of your region. One student should be elected to serve as secretary to fill out the form provided by the teacher. Share the information you have found with the rest of the group as the secretary takes notes.

*Targeted Standards and Reflection*

1.1 **Interpersonal Communication**: Students work in groups to organize geographical and cultural information in French.
1.2 **Interpretive Communication**: Students read and interpret authentic documents in French about their region.
2.1 **Practice of Culture**: Students learn about various cultural practices while consulting authentic documents in French.

2.2 **Products of Culture**: Students learn about various cultural products while consulting authentic documents in French.

3.1 **Making Connections**: Students increase their knowledge of a region of France.

3.2 **Acquiring Information**: Students use authentic documents from the Internet to learn about a region of France.

The teacher collects and verifies the master forms for completeness and accuracy, and copies are made for each member of the group and for the teacher.

### *Weeks 5-8: Summary*

Each group selects four Francophone countries from a list provided by the teacher.[3] Following the same procedures used earlier, students locate recipes and find specific geographic and cultural information about each of the countries. Students can work individually or in pairs but should exchange countries within the group when working on the two parts so that each member is exposed to some aspect of all four countries.

For each country, students should find (1) the capital, (2) the country's topology, (3) the population, (4) the largest city, (5) the date of independence, (6) the head of state, (7-8) two historical facts, (9) one famous person native to the country, and (10) a food or agricultural product for which the country is known. They must also find (11) a map, (12) a flag, (13) an image of the largest city, and (14-15) pictures of two monuments or geographic features.

### *Week 9*

Each group selects a menu that includes one course from each of the four Francophone countries and one from a region of France. The teacher distributes a handout with useful vocabulary and expressions in the form of a questionnaire: *Is this a light or heavy dish? Is it fried? Boiled? Baked? What is the preparation time? Should the dish be refrigerated before serving? Do the* hors d'oeuvre *go well with the soup? Do the vegetables go with the main course? Could you eat a dessert after this meal?*[4] This handout also helps students organize their discussion of the recipes for each course. In order to arrive at the final selections, students need to explain their responses within their group and make comparisons among the other dishes.

### *Assignment*

Take the recipes your group has collected and compose your own menu for a Francophone meal with one course (appetizer, soup, main course, vegetable, dessert) coming from each of the four Francophone countries and a region of France. Imagine a meal that is well balanced, can be prepared given the time and facilities you have available, will keep well between preparation and judging, and will be interesting to eat. For the five recipes you choose, make sure you are familiar with each of the ingredients.

In your group during class time, use the questionnaire provided by your teacher to discuss your choices. Decide upon a complete five-course menu for your group.

*Targeted Standards and Reflection*

1.1 **Interpersonal Communication**: Students work together to select a Francophone menu.
1.2 **Interpretive Communication**: Students read and interpret recipes in French.
2.1 **Practices of Culture**: Students reflect on cultural practices in selecting a menu.
2.2 **Products of Culture**: Students learn about some products of Francophone cultures.

The teacher should check the menus to see that they conform to the selection criteria and make suggestions where necessary. Copies are made for each member of the group and for the teacher.

### *Weeks 10-12: Summary*

Students carefully study the five recipes they have chosen, learning vocabulary for new food items, utensils, and cooking techniques. In the recipes, students identify verbs that describe cooking techniques and illustrate them with photos or drawings. A local chef can present a demonstration for the class, or area residents from some of the Francophone countries selected can speak about the eating customs in their culture. Students search for recipes in English for similar dishes and compare the way recipes are written in the two languages. Finally, each group chooses the dish they wish to prepare for the contest. Depending on the number of groups, the teacher should ensure that all five courses are represented and that there is no duplication. All of the Standards' goals can be targeted in these activities as noted below.

*Targeted Standards and Reflection*

1.1 **Interpersonal Communication**: Students work in groups to discuss recipes and food preparation.
1.2 **Interpretive Communication**: Students read and interpret recipes in French and listen to guest speakers.
1.3 **Presentational Communication**: Students prepare illustrations that reflect French cooking techniques and complete assignments based on the recipes.
2.1 **Practices of Culture**: Students learn about cooking techniques and eating habits in French from authentic documents and guest speakers.
2.2 **Products of Culture**: Students learn about foods and dishes from Francophone countries.
3.1 **Making Connections**: Students further their knowledge of cooking techniques.

3.2 **Acquiring Information**: Students use the Internet and contact native speakers to learn about French and Francophone cooking techniques and eating habits.

4.1 **Linguistic Comparisons**: Students compare the language used to describe food in English and in French.

4.2 **Cultural Comparisons**: Students compare the format of recipes written in French and in English and develop an appreciation for the role of the cook or chef in each culture.

5.1 **School and Community**: Students use the language with guest speakers.

5.2 **Lifelong Learning**: Students show evidence of enjoying French and Francophone cuisines.

Several types of evaluation are possible. The teacher can prepare specific, non-objective activities and exercises for evaluative purposes. These might include rewriting a recipe using conjugated verbs instead of infinitives or vice versa or rewriting the recipe in the past tense. Students can show illustrations or prepare an in-class demonstration of the techniques used in preparing a recipe. They might also interview French natives or food professionals in and out of the classroom.

### *Week 13*

Each group prepares a plan for making one of the dishes. The teacher prepares and distributes a form to help students organize the information. If necessary, students can enlist the cooperation of parents or people with expertise in cooking.

### *Assignment*

Each member of the group will perform a different task that will result in a plan for making and presenting a dish at the contest. One student prepares a shopping list of ingredients with approximate prices. Another makes a list of the utensils and equipment needed and where they are available. A third student creates a timetable for preparing the dish—from buying ingredients to serving the finished product. The fourth student assigns specific tasks to each member of the group, such as shopping, chopping or measuring ingredients, cooking, or preparing the presentation of the dish.

In your group during class time, choose one member of the group to serve as secretary and complete the form provided by your teacher. Students should perform different tasks and present their decisions to the rest of the group as the secretary takes notes.

*Targeted Standards and Reflection*

1.1 **Interpersonal Communication**: Students work in groups to organize the preparation of their recipe.
1.2 **Interpretive Communication**: Students read and interpret a recipe in French.
2.1 **Practices of Culture**: Students reflect on cultural practices in planning their contest entry.
2.2 **Products of Culture**: Students reflect on cultural products in planning their contest entry.

The teacher collects and evaluates the plans and makes suggestions where necessary. Copies are made for each member of the group and for the teacher.

### Weeks 14-16

The groups organize the contest and contact potential judges and guests. Each group receives an assignment related to the contest. Some of these must be carried out in English. Those groups with English assignments must report orally each week in French to the class as indicated. Tasks include (1) selecting a date, time, and location; (2) identifying potential judges and contacting them; (3) establishing rules and judging criteria; (4) determining award categories and prizes; (5) planning activities that follow the judging; and (6) publicizing the event.

*Assignment*

**Group 1**: In consultation with your teacher, select a date, time, and location for the contest. Check the school calendar and survey your classmates for potential conflicts. Determine what facilities are needed for the contest itself and any activity to follow, and choose an appropriate location. Check with school authorities to find out what sort of permission is required. You will need to consult with Group 5 about the activities that will follow the contest. In French, prepare a weekly oral report (3 to 4 minutes) and a final written report (one-half page) to communicate your decisions to the class.

**Group 2**: In consultation with your teacher and classmates, compose a list of school administrators, school board members, other teachers, community members, native speakers, or parents who might be willing to serve as judges. Others can be invited guests. Try to identify people with connections to French or to cooking. Contact people on the list to find three or four individuals who are willing to participate and are available on the date chosen. Consult with Group 1 about the date. Prepare letters of invitation in English. Using the model given by your teacher, prepare invitations in French containing the same information. Do not try to translate the English letter. Send the letters to those who have agreed to be judges.

**Group 3**: Prepare a list of rules for the contest and determine judging criteria. You should have four to six rules regarding the preparation and presentation of the recipe. There should be three to five criteria on which the entries will be judged. Then prepare a judging sheet in English with a well-defined scale as well as a list of rules for participants that is written in French. Base your decisions as much as possible on what you know of French cuisine and its traditions. Prepare an oral report (5 minutes) describing your decisions, to be presented in French to the rest of the class.

**Group 4**: Select descriptive categories for awards in addition to an overall Best Entry. There should be five or six different categories. Work with Group 3 to add these categories to the judging form. Base your decisions as much as possible on what you know of French cuisine and its traditions. Prepare an oral report in French (5 minutes) on your selections to present to the rest of the class. In consultation with your teacher, decide whether or not prizes or certificates will be awarded, and begin to solicit or prepare them.

**Group 5**: In consultation with your teacher and Group 1, decide what sort of event will follow the contest itself. Will it be a tasting or a meal? Who will be invited? How many people will attend? Determine what sort of facilities will be needed based on your decisions. This will also influence the quantity of each dish that must be prepared and whether other items will be served. Therefore, you may also need to consult with Group 3 regarding the contest rules. Prepare an oral and written report in French to communicate your decisions to the class (5 minutes).

**Group 6**: In consultation with the other groups and your teacher, decide on a publicity campaign for the contest. The event should be announced in at least three different ways. Prepare an oral report in French (5 minutes) for the class describing your plan. The results of the contest must also be publicized afterwards. Arrange for photos to be taken.

*Targeted Standards and Reflection*

1.1 **Interpersonal Communication**: Students work in groups to discuss plans for the contest.
1.3 **Presentation Communication**: Students prepare oral and written reports and documents in French based on their group work.
2.1 **Practices of Culture**: Students demonstrate knowledge of cultural practices in preparing for the contest and in composing documents.
4.2 **Cultural Comparisons**: Students make comparisons between French and English attitudes toward cuisine in preparing documents and rules for the contest.
5.1 **School and Community**: Students use the language outside the classroom.

The teacher collects and evaluates the documents, checking for any potential problems. The teacher evaluates oral presentations. Copies of all reports and forms are made for each class member and the teacher.

### *Weeks 17-18: Summary*

Students prepare for the event itself. Each group is assigned a task including: (1) making a list of items needed, jobs to be done, and who will handle them; (2) creating certificates and soliciting prizes; (3) preparing a guest list and invitations for guests; (4) creating menus and place cards; (5) decorating the room. Each group should make two illustrated posters highlighting the Francophone countries or regions of France studied, and these will be used as decoration for the room during the contest.

### *Week 19: Summary*

The contest takes place and prizes are awarded. Group 6 follows up with publicity on the winners.

### *Weeks 20-24: Summary*

Students prepare the class Francophone "cookbook." Each group can produce its own printed cookbook, and these might then be compiled. Each group might take on a different task for the preparation of a class cookbook, selecting format, editing recipes, editing cultural materials, organizing illustrations, etc. Cookbooks can also be produced on-line as Web pages and illustrated with photos from the contest. During the final week, the class produces and distributes its cookbook. Each of the judges and invited guests should receive a copy of the cookbook, a note of appreciation for their participation, and a copy of any news clippings.

## Conclusion

Long-term, content-based projects based on authentic documents offer several advantages. The thoroughness with which a topic can be explored over many weeks suits the multidisciplinary and multifaceted nature of the Standards' goals. Projects provide a context for language and cultural learning that can motivate students in their study of a language. When authentic documents are used, students realize very quickly that they can utilize their knowledge of the target language to acquire, interpret, and discuss information. The unedited recipes and related materials in this project allow students to make their own observations and apply what they already know about cuisine in order to draw new conclusions regarding Francophone cultures. In addition to motivation and cultural awareness, this type of project provides a unifying factor to the often discrete grammar, vocabulary, and culture items of a textbook and helps create a sense of community in the classroom. Finally, the public event of the contest is a reward for the students' efforts, and the cookbook itself is a tangible reminder of their accomplishments.

## Notes

[1]   Some portions of the project are summarized here. A complete lesson plan as excerpted here can be found on the AATF Web site at <http://aatf.utsa.edu/general/cscart.htm>.

[2]   Common French search engines are Nomade <http://www.nomade.fr> and Yahoo! France <http://www.yahoo.fr>.

[3]   The teacher may wish to check Web sites first to determine what is available for the various Francophone countries and eliminate from the list any countries about which little information can be found.

[4]   A sample menu would be: (1) Appetizer: *Accras de morue* (Cod fritters) from Guadeloupe (2) Soup: *Soupe à l'ail* (Garlic soup) from the Languedoc-Roussillon region in France; (3) Main course: *Poulet farci au couscous doux* (Stuffed chicken with sweet couscous) from Morocco; (4) Vegetable: *Beignets d'aubergines* (Fried eggplant) from Mauritius; (5) Dessert: *Tartelette à l'érable* (Maple tart) from Quebec.

## References

Jourdain, S. (1998). Building connections to culture: A student-centered approach. *Foreign Language Annals, 31* (3), 437-447.

Lee, L. (1997). Using Internet tools as an enhancement of C2 teaching and learning. *Foreign Language Annals, 30* (3), 410-425.

National Standards in Foreign Language Education Project. (1999). *Standards for Foreign Language Learning in the 21st Century.* Lawrence, KS: Allen Press.

Robinson-Stuart, G. & Nocon, H. (1996). Second culture acquisition: Ethnography in the foreign language classroom. *The Modern Language Journal, 80* (iv), 431-449.

Turnbull, M. (1999). Multidimensional project-based teaching in French second language (FSL): A process-product case study. *The Modern Language Journal, 83* (iv), 548-568.

Walz, J. (1998). Meeting standards for foreign language learning with World Wide Web activities. *Foreign Language Annals, 31* (1), 103-114.

# 4
# Supporting and Sustaining Change: The *MICH-I-LIFTS* Project

**Anne Nerenz**
Eastern Michigan University

**Emily Spinelli**
University of Michigan, Dearborn

**Cindy Kendall**
Michigan State University

**JoAnne Wilson**
Glen Arbor, MI

**Tom Lovik**
Michigan State University

**Jackie Moase-Burke**
Oakland (MI) Public Schools

During the last 30 years, the foreign language profession has undergone rapid change. Emphasis on linguistic proficiency, a growing awareness of differences in learning styles, the emergence of state and national standards, and the widespread availability of new technologies have had a profound impact on what, how, and whom we teach. District-wide in-service opportunities and focused programming at state and regional foreign language conferences offer opportunities to expose language professionals to changing philosophies, curricula, and instructional methods. However, sustaining change in curriculum, instruction, and assessment to the point that these changes become standard teaching practice requires a focused and continuous commitment to professional development. In Michigan, the *Mich-I-Lifts (Michigan Improving Language Instruction for Teachers and Students)* project was designed to provide such longer-term support. This professional development program offered a series of intensive teacher institutes, workshops, interactive video-conferences, and on-line mentoring over a period of two and one-half years (October 1999–May 2002). The project sought to improve the quality of K-12 foreign language instruction in Michigan by working continuously with a cadre of teachers who were committed to modeling best practice in their classrooms and implementing change within their schools and school districts. The project was a collaborative effort of the Michigan Department of Education and the Michigan Foreign Language Association. It was funded through a Foreign Language Assistance Project (FLAP) grant.

Once funding was awarded in June 1999, project descriptions and application forms were mailed to schools, school districts, and intermediate school districts throughout the state. This professional development opportunity was also announced through the Michigan Foreign Language Association Newsletter, and an initial cadre of 62 French, Spanish, German, and Japanese teachers made a commitment to the project. In order to insure that these teachers would be able to participate in each scheduled activity, participants' district administrators were also required to submit a letter of commitment agreeing (1) to support the teacher in his or her efforts to implement new technologies and standards-based curriculum and assessments, and (2) to release the participant throughout the duration of the grant to attend project workshops, both days of the state foreign language association annual meeting, and the video-conference. Although district support was confirmed at the beginning of the project and although teachers were asked to make a long-term commitment to the project, the number of participants was reduced for a variety of personal or professional reasons in each subsequent year— from 62 in October 1999, to 42 in October 2000, and 31 in October 2001. As these numbers point out, one of the obstacles to initiating and sustaining change in a long-term effort like *Mich-I-Lifts* is maintaining a committed and consistent community of learners throughout the duration of the project.

**An Overview to the Project**

*Mich-I-Lifts* had different major objectives during each year of the project. Activities in Year 1 were designed to (1) familiarize teachers with state and national standards, (2) acquaint teachers with new technologies, and (3) support teachers in their efforts to improve their own proficiency in the target language. The major objective of Year 1 was to help participants develop and implement a Personal Professional Plan (PPP) in which they stated their goals in each of the three major areas. During the first year of the project, participants attended a full-day workshop held immediately prior to the Michigan Foreign Language Association annual conference; participated in technology, standards-based, or language-specific workshops of their choice funded by the project at that conference; established on-line mentoring relationships with peers and project leaders; and attended a two-day intensive institute during the summer. At the end of Year 1, participants submitted a written summary of the goals they had achieved and discussed their PPP with their mentor. An overview to *Mich-I-Lifts* activities during Year 1 is provided in the following table.

## OVERVIEW TO YEAR ONE

| Date | Standards Implementation | Language Improvement | Technology |
|------|-------------------------|---------------------|------------|
| October 1999 | Comparison of state and national standards<br><br>Standards self-assessment | Overview to the proficiency movement and OPI rating scales<br><br>Proficiency self-assessment<br><br>Language-specific sessions with native speakers | Introduction to e-mail and e-group listserve<br><br>Technology self-assessment |
| October - December 1999 | Development of Personal Professional Plan: Standards implementation goals | Development of Personal Professional Plan: Language improvement goals | Development of Personal Professional Plan: Technology goals for personal and professional use |
| January – May 2000 | Implementation of standards goals in curriculum and daily lesson plans | Implementation of language improvement goals | Implementation of technology goals |
| Summer 2000 | Review of standards implementation goals with mentor | Review of language improvement goals with mentor<br><br>Language-specific sessions with native speakers | Review of technology goals with mentor |

The major objective of Year 2 was to help participants develop and refine a learning scenario, lesson plans, and an assessment rubric on a topic of their choice. Participants were encouraged to implement their scenario with their students during Year 2 of the project. During the second year of the project, participants attended a full-day workshop held immediately prior to the Michigan Foreign Language Association annual conference, participated in at least one technology workshop at that conference funded by the project, attended a mid-year video-conference, participated in on-line mentoring relationships with peers and project leaders, and attended a 2-day intensive institute during the summer. These activities are summarized below.

**OVERVIEW TO YEAR 2**

| Date | Activity |
|---|---|
| October 2000 | Introduction to assessment<br>Introduction to and analysis of learning scenarios<br>Language-specific sessions with native speakers |
| January 2001 | Description of learning scenario submitted to mentor<br>    for feedback<br>Revision of learning scenario description |
| February 2001 | Videoconference: Presentation of learning scenarios by<br>    two participants followed by whole group discussion<br>    and small group question/answer<br>Scenario guidelines and templates reviewed and refined |
| April  2001 | Completed learning scenario templates posted to Web site<br>    for peer review |
| Summer 2001 | Two-day intensive institutes focusing on assessment and<br>    writing rubrics, peer-mentoring, and review of<br>    learning scenario with mentor<br>Language-specific sessions with native speakers |
| September 2001 | Learning scenarios, lesson plans, and assessment rubric<br>    reviewed by mentor |
| October 2001 | Small-group presentations of revised scenarios<br>Peer review of revised scenarios<br>On-going meetings with mentors and editors<br>Language-specific sessions with native speakers |
| June 2002 | Publication of learning scenarios<br>End of project celebration with participants and their<br>    district administrators |

**Year 1: Developing and Enhancing Fundamental Skills**

Once a cadre of teachers was identified and letters of support from their school districts were secured, Year 1 of the project began with a full-day workshop devoted to helping teachers assess their skills and prepare a personalized professional development plan. Instruction and self-assessments were completed in three areas: (1) standards familiarization and implementation, (2) language proficiency, and (3) knowledge and use of new technologies. Each of these areas and the activities that supported them are described below.

## Supporting the Standards Familiarization Goal

Because many Michigan teachers were unfamiliar with state and national standards for foreign language learning, the project was designed to improve teachers' knowledge of the standards and help them to develop and implement curriculum, instructional strategies, and assessments that were congruent with the standards, with current research, and with best practice. At the beginning of the project, participants were introduced to the *Michigan World Language Content Standards* (1998) and the *Standards for Foreign Language Learning in the 21st Century* (1999). Participants learned how and by whom the state and national standards were developed and drew parallels between state and national content areas and goals. As each standard was explained and illustrated, participants completed a self-assessment that addressed ways in which participants might implement the communications, culture, connections, comparisons, and communities goals (Nerenz, 1999). This self-assessment instrument is included as Appendix A.

Once participants had completed the instructional and self-assessment portions of the workshop, they created a PPP to guide their implementation of the national standards in the classroom during the coming year. Standards implementation goals that were planned in December and then reported as having been achieved at the close of Year 1 are shown in Table 1.

**TABLE 1: Standards Implementation Goals**

| Goal Area | Planned | Reported Achieved | Percent Reported Achieved |
|---|---|---|---|
| **Communication** | | | |
| Use more teacher foreign language | 11 | 6 | |
| Have students present information on topics of personal interest | 1 | 1 | |
| Provide increased opportunities for interpersonal, interpretive, and presentational communication, including role plays, scenarios, information-gap activities, and authentic children's books | 11 | 7 | |
| **Total Communication Goals** | **23** | **14** | **61%** |
| **Culture** | | | |
| Collect and use realia and culturally authentic products and materials | 8 | 4 | |
| Develop lessons that focus on products, practices, and perspectives | 1 | 1 | |
| **Total Culture Goals** | **9** | **5** | **56%** |

| Connections | | | |
|---|---|---|---|
| Enrich the curriculum with content from other content areas | 7 | 7 | |
| **Total Connections Goals** | **7** | **7** | **100%** |
| **Comparisons** | | | |
| Develop lessons that promote cultural comparisons | 4 | 4 | |
| **Total Comparisons Goals** | **4** | **4** | **100%** |
| **Communities** | | | |
| Expose students to native speakers or topic specialists in the community | 6 | 3 | |
| Offer regular opportunities for meaningful use of language in and out of the classroom | 5 | 4 | |
| **Total Communities Goals** | **11** | **7** | **64%** |

As shown in this table, participants identified a total of 58 goals and reported having achieved 37 (68%). Nearly twice as many goals were identified in the area of communications as in the areas of culture, connections, comparisons, or communities. While fewer participants listed goals in the areas of connections and comparisons, the 100% achievement rate indicates that these participants also reported great success in accomplishing them.

**Supporting the Language Improvement Goal**

Current emphasis on the exclusive use of the target language in the classroom requires that teachers have strong language skills. However, many teachers in Michigan work essentially in isolation because of the size of the state and the existence of many rural communities. Thus, it is difficult or impossible for teachers to interact in the target language with native or otherwise fluent speakers or to use the language they teach for real communication. Activities during Year 1 of the *Mich-I-Lifts* project were designed to help participants improve their language proficiency. In an effort to support participants' language improvement, small group sessions with native speakers were included at all workshops and summer institutes. In order to help participants understand and begin to assess their own command of the target language, a segment of the project's initial workshop was devoted to familiarizing participants with the notion of proficiency and the contributions to a proficiency rating made by one's ability to carry out linguistic functions in a variety of contexts with a particular level of grammatical accuracy. During the proficiency familiarization session, participants reviewed the history and development of the proficiency movement as well as the *ACTFL Proficiency Guidelines* (1986). After working with shorthand descriptions for each proficiency level, participants completed a language proficiency self-assessment (Spinelli, 2001). This assessment instrument is included as Appendix B.

Having completed the proficiency self-assessment, participants were asked to add to their PPPs a set of language improvement goals to guide their professional development efforts during the next 12 months. Participants' progress toward those goals was reported during the summer institutes. The total number of language improvement goals set by project participants is shown in Table 2.

**Table 2: Language Improvement Goals**

| Goal Area | Planned | Reported Achieved | Percent Achieved |
|---|---|---|---|
| **Linguistic Function** | | | |
| Improve ability to construct and develop hypotheses | 2 | 0 | |
| Improve ability to express and support opinions | 4 | 1 | |
| **Total** | **6** | **1** | **17%** |
| **Grammatical Accuracy** | | | |
| Improve grammatical competence | 5 | 1 | |
| **Total** | **5** | **1** | **20%** |
| **Contexts or Content Areas** | | | |
| Increase vocabulary base (learn specialized business and technical vocabulary, slang, or vocabulary related to elementary content and curriculum) | 8 | 2 | |
| Increase number of contexts and registers in which I am able to speak | 5 | 0 | |
| Improve knowledge of current events | 3 | 3 | |
| Deal with unfamiliar topics | 3 | 0 | |
| **Total** | **19** | **5** | **26%** |
| **Practice Opportunities** | | | |
| Complete the AP Spanish practice book and CD ROM programs | 1 | 0 | |
| Enroll in a Master of Arts program | 1 | 1 | |
| Study abroad or travel abroad with students | 3 | 3 | |
| Read news browsers, Web sources, magazines, newspapers, and novels. Complete daily school-wide silent Spanish reading activities | 7 | 7 | |
| Join a Spanish book discussion group, a chat group, or an e-mail group | 2 | 3 | |
| Watch Univision and the International Channel | 1 | 1 | |
| Use target language for pleasure; attend community events or mass in Spanish | 1 | 1 | |
| E-mail native speaker friends | 1 | 1 | |
| Make contact with exchange students and native speakers in community | 6 | 3 | |
| **Total** | **23** | **20** | **87%** |

It is interesting to observe that participants who framed their goals in terms of linguistic functions, grammatical accuracy, or context-specific vocabulary reported being less successful than participants who stated their goals in terms of specific opportunities to use and practice the language. Clearly, it is much easier to participate in a study abroad program, join a language-specific book club, or e-mail native speaker friends than it is to master the expressions and grammar needed to hypothesize or support one's opinions effectively.

**Supporting the Technology Goal**

Because many teachers lacked familiarity with new technologies–including e-mail and the Internet, scanners, digital photography, and PowerPoint–and confidence to use them, the project was designed to formalize and expand participants' use of technology as an instructional tool, as a professional resource, and as a means of participating in the project itself. During the technology familiarization sessions, participants completed a technology self-assessment (Kendall, 1999, Appendix C) and learned how to use e-mail and to register with the *Mich-I-Lifts* e-group. In addition to participating in regular on-line mentoring and submitting their work electronically throughout the year, participants also elected to attend either a PowerPoint workshop or a WebQuests workshop during the Year 1 summer institute.

Participants' technology goals were described in their PPPs, and progress toward those goals was reported during the summer institutes. A summary of participants' technology goals is shown in Table 3.

**Table 3: Technology Goals**

| Goal Area | Planned | Reported Achieved | Percent Reported Achieved |
|---|---|---|---|
| **Develop skills and use new technology** | | | |
| *Developing Basic Skills* | | | |
| Become comfortable with word-processing | 5 | 2 | |
| Learn to make charts and graphs | 1 | 1 | |
| Learn to use clip art | 2 | 1 | |
| Learn to use textbook CD ROM | 2 | 1 | |
| Learn to use a grading program | 3 | 3 | |
| Use TV5 and Univision in the classroom | 2 | 1 | |
| **Enhancing Technology Skills** | | | |
| Learn to use a digital camera | 4 | 4 | |
| Learn to use a scanner | 5 | 2 | |
| Learn, and teach students to use, PowerPoint | 15 | 7 | |
| Use HyperStudio | 3 | 2 | |
| Learn to set up interactive video conferences | 1 | 0 | |
| Create or refine a personal Web page | 6 | 4 | |
| Digitize audio and video | 1 | 1 | |
| **Total** | **50** | **29** | **58%** |

| | | | |
|---|---|---|---|
| **Use Electronic Communication Services** | | | |
| Use e-mail and Instant Messenger | 10 | 6 | |
| Understand and use the project e-group | 2 | 2 | |
| Set up e-pals with schools abroad or with | | | |
| an American school | 6 | 5 | |
| **Total** | **18** | **13** | **72%** |
| | | | |
| **Explore the Internet** | | | |
| Learn to use search engines to make | | | |
| scrapbook lists of favorite sites | 19 | 14 | |
| Use automated news sites | 1 | 1 | |
| Download authentic materials and visuals | 5 | 2 | |
| Use virtual tours in lessons | | | |
| **Total** | **26** | **17** | **65%** |
| | | | |
| **Total Technology Goals** | **94** | **59** | **63%** |

As Table 3 shows, participants elected to pursue a very large number of technology goals. They identified a total of 94 technology goals, compared with 54 standards implementation goals and 53 language improvement goals. These technology goals were distributed across three main areas: (1) developing new skills and using new technologies, (2) using e-mail, and (3) exploring the Internet. These data also show that 33 of the 94 technology goals (35%) involved developing basic technological skills or learning to use e-mail.

### Comparing Year 1 Goals

It is interesting that these Michigan teachers identified more than 40 ways to make changes in their teaching and that, as a group, they considered implementing more than 200 strategies for enhancing students' language learning experiences. It is also striking that *Mich-I-Lifts* participants reported having achieved more than half of the goals they listed in each of the three areas. Self-reported data show that participants were most successful in putting into practice their standards implementation goals (68% reported achieved) and their technology goals (63%), compared with 47% of their language improvement goals.

### Year 2: Focusing on Learning Scenarios and Assessment

Activities during the second year of the project focused on sustaining and strengthening the changes initiated during Year 1 and on helping participants to prepare, refine, and pilot test an original learning scenario. In order to complete this task, participants needed to (1) understand fundamental principles of evaluation, (2) be able to distinguish between a classroom activity and a learning scenario, (3) select a scenario topic that would be interesting, age-appropriate, and relevant to their students and their curriculum, (4) complete and refine a description of their scenario using a standardized template, (5) develop detailed lesson plans, and 6) prepare an assessment instrument. Although it is beyond the scope of this paper to provide detailed examples of participants' scenarios, their work will be disseminated through the Michigan Foreign Language Association and posted at <http://www.klick.org/michilifts> on the *Mich-I-Lifts* Web site in late 2002.

### Defining and Developing the Scenario

Before participants could develop a learning scenario, it was important that they distinguish it from a more typical classroom activity. For the purpose of the *Mich-I-Lifts* project, a learning scenario was defined as an extended thematic unit from which students developed a product, a presentation, original research, or other project on a high-interest and age-appropriate topic of their choice. The scenario had to allow language learners to develop and demonstrate interpersonal, interpretive, and presentational language skills while gathering and sharing information from the point of view of both the native and target cultures. Students were required to demonstrate a variety of technological, interpersonal, investigative, and academic skills. They were also expected to show that they had contacted members of a living language community, used authentic target language materials, and learned and incorporated content from other disciplines. These components and requirements were incorporated into the *Mich-I-Lifts* scenario template.

Before developing their own scenarios, participants analyzed sample scenarios from the *Standards for Foreign Language Learning in the 21ˢᵗ Century* (1999), first listing and categorizing what students would need to know and be able to do, then noting the skills students would need to work together successfully, and finally listing and categorizing the specific skills as well as linguistic, cultural, and content knowledge that students would need in order to complete the task. The resulting lists were quite daunting. Participants quickly realized that a learning scenario is infinitely more complex and distinctly different from typical sequences of classroom activities that demand only that students show control of a limited amount of vocabulary or a defined set of grammatical rules, that require students to use a selective set of skills, that focus all students on the same topic at the same time, and that are carried out over a relatively brief period.

### Lesson Plans and Assessments

Once participants had developed and refined the description of their learning scenarios using the uniform scenario template, they prepared either daily lesson plans for scenarios that could be completed in one to two weeks or weekly plans for scenarios lasting three weeks or more. Completed plans took into account the proficiency level of the students; the amount of total class time involved; the accessibility of materials, equipment, and technology; and the relationship between in-class and out-of-class activities. In their plans, participants outlined lesson objectives, noted what students would already need to know and be able to do in order to begin the project, and stated new functions, vocabulary, or grammar to be learned, as appropriate. Participants also listed students' and teachers' use of technology, described the sequence of activities, and referenced these activities to the national standards project.

Participants also planned three kinds of assessments. Homework assignments as well as interim written and oral activities were used to verify students' understanding of basic language functions, vocabulary, and structures. Students were also graded on the timelines and thoroughness of each component of the project, and, for group projects, on their reliability, commitment, and interactions within the group. Finally, participants designed a means to evaluate students' final products.

## On-line Mentoring

Sustaining change in teachers' beliefs, attitudes, objectives, and teaching behaviors required more frequent contact than the formally-scheduled, on-site meetings could provide. While the workshops, video-conference, and summer institutes helped to build group cohesiveness and provided opportunities for hands-on or language-specific instruction, on-line mentoring enabled peers and team leaders to provide more continuous day-to-day support for teachers' professional development efforts. From the beginning, participants in the *Mich-I-Lifts* project used e-mail almost continuously to solicit advice and input from their mentors and reported using e-mail regularly to communicate with other project participants. Similarly, mentors used electronic communication to comment on individual participants' self-improvement plans, scenario topics, lesson plans, and assessment rubrics. While there is no statistical record of the frequency with which participants and their mentors used e-mail to communicate directly with a particular individual, mentors and participants both agreed that the project could not have been conducted without such electronic technology.

In addition, the *Mich-I-Lifts* project relied on two sites on the Web: a public site that provided information about project goals, timelines, and faculty mentors <http://www.klick.org/michilifts> and a private site, accessible only to authorized *Mich-I-Lifts* mentors and participants. Project participants used the private site to send messages to the whole group, chat with other members, save files remotely, download templates, share a common calendar, vote for preferred institute dates or seminar locations, and post their Personal Professional Plans (PPPs), learning scenarios, and other assignments. The e-group permitted participants to pose questions to the entire group and to seek specific feedback both on their work within the project as well as on questions of professional interest.

During the 2-year period described in this article, 663 messages were posted by group participants through the e-group site. During Year 1, all leaders were accessible and available to all participants, and often several different mentors would respond to an individual message posted to the e-group. While this type of whole group communication was continued in Year 2, participants were also divided into small groups and directly assigned to a mentor. This change offered increased opportunities for consistent, focused, and individualized coaching and accountability.

A summary of the topics addressed through the listserve is provided in Table 4.

**Table 4: Messages posted by Participants and Mentors**

| Topic | Messages Initiated by Participants | Messages Initiated by Mentors | % of Total Messages |
|---|---|---|---|
| **Project Administration** (assignments, dates, stipends, …) | 85 | 74 | 24% |
| **Queries on specific topics** | 127 | 31 | 24% |
| Pre-K and elementary language learning | 18 | 7 | |
| Useful Web sites | 18 | 1 | |
| Texts, materials, and curriculum | 14 | 8 | |
| Working with student teachers, new teachers, and certification issues | 11 | 1 | |
| Homework and exams | 7 | 3 | |
| Travel and study abroad programs | 7 | - | |
| Developing a personal Web page | 6 | 1 | |
| Distance learning | 6 | 5 | |
| Foreign languages in Middle Schools | 5 | - | |
| Using foreign video | 4 | - | |
| Block scheduling | 4 | - | |
| Split-level classes | 2 | - | |
| **Other topics** | 25 | 5 | |
| **Managing Technology and Posting Assignments** | 41 | 106 | 22% |
| **On-line Introductions** | 97 | 40 | 21% |
| **Information on Resources and Opportunities** | 30 | 32 | 9% |
| **Total Messages** | 380 | 283 | |

As shown in Table 4, approximately one quarter of the total messages posted to the site involved administrative issues (dates, stipends, agendas, etc.) and another 22% were requests for help, primarily involving assignments and technological issues. In a large project such as *Mich-I-Lifts*, processing all of these requests using more conventional means would have been costly as well as overwhelmingly time-consuming. More than half of the total messages were initiated by participants, and one-third of those messages requested specific help or information and led to the formation of electronic conversation groups on topics of professional interest, as illustrated by the messages reprinted below.

> From KL, 11/9/1999: I teach 4th and 5th year French at ... High School, and unfortunately we do not have a written curriculum at this time. I am pretty much on my own, therefore, with no textbook. I would be glad to get together sometime and discuss how I am dealing with this!
>
> From SF, 12/8/1999 I am going crazy this year with a French 2/3 split class and new texts. Any good ideas would be greatly appreciated. I only have 13 in Fr 3 and I'm afraid I'm losing a lot of them because they have to work on their own a lot.

Participants also used the listserve to announce professional development opportunities and to call attention to especially interesting teaching resources or Web sites. It is clear from the type and number of messages that this component of the project was frequently used and enormously successful. Indeed, in a large state like Michigan where there are many isolated and rural school districts, a project like *Mich-I-Lifts* simply could not have been efficiently administered, and teachers' efforts to learn, experiment with, and implement new teaching strategies could not have been effectively supported without the opportunities offered by the on-line, electronic network.

## Conclusion

District-wide in-service sessions and state or regional conferences have traditionally provided and will continue to offer rich and engaging professional development opportunities for foreign language teachers. Participants often leave such workshops with a wealth of new teaching strategies and materials as well as a renewed eagerness to try out these ideas with their students. In addition to such annual or semi-annual opportunities to share with and learn from each other, teachers also need long-term opportunities to gather with peers to reconsider the more fundamental elements of their teaching philosophy and classroom practice. Thanks to *FLAP* grant funding as well as support from the Michigan Department of Education and the Michigan Foreign Language Association, foreign language teachers in Michigan were able to engage in sustained professional development and to put into practice a new vision of how, what, and whom we teach.

## References

American Council on the Teaching of Foreign Languages. (1986). *Proficiency guidelines*. Yonkers, NY: Author.

Kendall, C. (1999). *Technology self-assessment*. Unpublished assessment instrument. East Lansing, MI: Michigan State University.

Michigan Department of Education. (1998). *Michigan world language content standards*. Lansing, MI: Author.

National Standards in Foreign Language Education Project. (1999). *Standards for foreign language learning in the 21st century*. Lawrence, KS: Allen Press.

Nerenz, A. G. (1999). *Standards self-assessment*. Unpublished assessment instrument. Ypsilanti, MI: Eastern Michigan University.

Spinelli, E. (2001). *Language self-assessment*. Unpublished assessment instrument. Dearborn, MI: University of Michigan, Dearborn.

## APPENDIX A
### Standards Self-Assessment (Nerenz, 1999)

**Communications** – Do I...
_____ 1. use the language for real communication in my personal life?
_____ 2. model interpersonal, interpretive, and presentational uses of language?
_____ 3. use the language consistently with students, tailoring my language to their level?
_____ 4. offer students regular opportunities for meaningful, interpersonal use of language?
_____ 5. offer students regular opportunities for meaningful pleasure and informational reading in the foreign language?
_____ 6. offer students regular opportunities to listen to the language both for pleasure and to gain new information?
_____ 7. offer students regular opportunities to present their ideas orally?
_____ 8. offer students regular opportunities to present their ideas in writing?
_____ 9. teach students how to use effective communication strategies?
_____ 10. present my students with materials from a variety of sources?

**Culture** – Do I...
_____ 1. model acceptance of, and interest in, cultures that are different from my own?
_____ 2. actively seek out opportunities to participate in cultural enrichment activities both at home and abroad?
_____ 3. seek out materials and build a developing collection of authentic resources?
_____ 4. relate daily lessons to an authentic cultural context?

_____  5.  actively develop students' knowledge of culturally-correct practices?

_____  6.  integrate a variety of culturally-authentic products (materials and artifacts) into each day's lesson?

_____  7.  help students to understand the culture's unique perspectives (values, points of view, and beliefs)?

_____  8.  focus on the wide variety of countries in which the language is used?

_____  9.  help students understand the variability among cultures and within a single culture so that students understand for whom the products, practices, and perspectives are true?

_____ 10.  develop and nurture relationships with colleagues that permit a sustained exchange of cultural materials and knowledge?

**Connections** – Do I...

_____  1.  use the foreign language to learn about new areas of personal interest?

_____  2.  use the International Channel, TV5, foreign news sites on the Web, magazines, and newspapers to keep in touch with foreign viewpoints?

_____  3.  integrate materials from non-textbook sources to expose students to alternative points of view?

_____  4.  expand the range of topics and activities beyond traditional grammatical rules, vocabulary, and "survival" situations?

_____  5.  feel comfortable "taking time out from the curriculum" to allow students to explore a hobby, activity, or topic of personal interest in the foreign language?

_____  6.  focus each lesson on interesting culture, content, or activities that add to students' background knowledge and "imagined" life-experience?

_____  7.  use the Internet?

_____  8.  have students use the Internet?

_____  9.  collaborate on a joint project with colleagues in another academic department?

_____ 10.  feel comfortable teaching or reinforcing content from "another subject area" ?

**Comparisons** – Do I...

_____  1.  understand the syntactical similarities and differences between English and the language I teach?

_____  2.  feel comfortable with the amount of grammar covered in the curriculum at each level (Level 1, Level 2, ...)?

_____  3.  prefer to teach grammar inductively (examples → rules) or deductively (rules → examples)?

_____  4.  believe that translation is important in helping students to compare L1 and L2?

_____  5.  teach students to observe, analyze, and compare vocabulary, idiomatic expressions, and language structures?

_____ 6.  help students **recognize** a cultural product and identify a comparable item in their own culture?

_____ 7.  offer students opportunities to **compare** products from different cultures?

_____ 8.  show students how to **use** a product, **carry out** an activity, or appropriately **execute** a series of actions and compare it to similar activities or procedures in their own culture?

_____ 9.  compare the value of the product, activity, or pattern of behavior in the culture being studied and in their own culture?

_____ 10.  help students understand that cultures fulfill the same fundamental human needs in different, but equally appropriate, ways?

**Community** – Do I…

_____ 1.  plan daily activities that allow students to exchange opinions, ideas, and new information with each other in meaningful and realistic ways?

_____ 2.  plan activities that connect students with others who learn or use the language outside of school?

_____ 3.  make the most of native speakers and the real and living presence of the language and culture in the communities in which we live?

_____ 4.  know of volunteer service-learning opportunities for language speakers in my community?

_____ 5.  stress the importance of foreign languages in the global community, marketplace, and workplace?

_____ 6.  allow students access to "kid-friendly" materials in the foreign language?

_____ 7.  integrate students' personal areas of interest into the curriculum and encourage them to pursue their interests in the foreign language?

_____ 8.  ask students to document their contact with or use of the foreign language outside of my classroom?

_____ 9.  plan lessons so that all students can experience success and develop increasing confidence, proficiency, and self-esteem?

_____ 10.  take pride in, and get satisfaction from, watching my students learn and grow; enjoy my content area, my students, and my position as a foreign language teacher?

## APPENDIX B

### Language Self-Assessment (Spinelli, 2001)

The following Language Self-Assessment is intended as an informal guide to help you rate yourself on a continuum from Novice – Intermediate – Advanced – Superior. The results are in no way scientific or official. For participants desiring a formal rating of their oral proficiency, they should contact the American Council on the Teaching of Foreign Languages (ACTFL) for an Oral Proficiency Interview given by a certified tester.

Rate yourself on your performance of the following linguistic tasks or functions. Write the number 3, 2, or 1 in front of each listed function according to the following key:     **3 = Always     2 = Sometimes     1 = Never**

1. ___ Able to list and enumerate
   *Examples: Able to list family members, the rooms of one's house or apartment, the items of clothing one is wearing, the food eaten for dinner*
2. ___ Able to speak using learned and memorized utterances
   *Examples: Uses standard phrases found in textbook dialogues and phrase lists*
3. ___ Able to speak using isolated words and/or phrases
4. ___ Intelligible to persons used to dealing with learners, language teachers
5. ___ Can create with language
   *Examples: Can go beyond learned or memorized utterances found in dialogues and phrase lists to formulate new utterances never seen or heard before*
6. ___ Can ask and answer questions
7. ___ Can open, sustain, and close a short conversation
8. ___ Can handle uncomplicated communicative tasks for survival in the target culture
   *Examples: Can order a meal in a restaurant; can make a routine purchase; can obtain lodging*
9. ___ Able to speak using isolated sentences
10. ___ Can communicate using predictable and concrete exchanges covering self, family, home, daily activities, interests, and personal preferences.
11. ___ Understandable to native speakers used to dealing with foreigners
    *Examples: Understandable to persons engaged in services related to tourism such as hotel, restaurant, or airport employees*
12. ___ Able to participate fully in conversations on a variety of topics relating to work, school, home, and leisure activities as well as to events of current, public, and personal interest

13. ___ Able to handle successfully the linguistic challenges presented by a complication or unexpected turn of events that occurs within the context of a routine situation
    *Examples: Can successfully return or exchange a faulty product; can replace a lost or stolen ticket*
14. ___ Can describe in detail
    *Examples: Can describe your living quarters, your job and its responsibilities, your best friend, or family members*
15. ___ Can narrate about current, past, and future activities
    *Examples: Can explain what you did last weekend; can explain what you used to do when you were in high school; can summarize a film, video, TV program, novel, article; can discuss a future activity such as a vacation*
16. ___ Communicates with paragraph-length connected discourse
17. ___ Understandable to native speakers not used to dealing with foreigners
18. ___ Can converse in formal and informal situations from both concrete and abstract perspectives
19. ___ Can tailor language to an audience
20. ___ Can deal with unfamiliar topics
21. ___ Can explain and support an opinion on a number of topics such as social and political issues
22. ___ Can construct and develop hypotheses to explore alternative possibilities
23. ___ Errors do not interfere with comprehension

## FINAL QUESTION

**Compared with my rating on the self-assessment taken in Fall 1999, my overall rating on this self assessment is  (Circle one)**

**HIGHER**               **SAME**               **LOWER**

## HOW TO SCORE THIS SELF-ASSESSMENT
In order to rate yourself on the proficiency scale you will need to find the area where you are always able to complete the tasks listed and the area where you are never able to complete the tasks listed.

1. Determine the number of the answer(s) where there is a change from "always" to "sometimes" in your responses. Make note of that number.
2. Determine the number of the answer(s) where there is a change from "sometimes" to "never" in your responses. Make note of that number.
3. Your rating will lie in the range between the end of the "always" answers and the beginning of the "never" answers.

Use the following key to the numbers of the responses to help you determine your rating.

| | |
|---|---|
| 1 – 4 | Novice Level Descriptions |
| 5 – 11 | Intermediate Level Descriptions |
| 12 – 17 | Advanced Level Descriptions |
| 18 – 23 | Superior Level Descriptions |

EXAMPLE: If the majority of your answers from 1-15 were "always" and the answers to questions 16-17 were "sometimes" and your answers beginning with 18 were "never," you would rank yourself an "ADVANCED."

© 2001 Emily Spinelli.  Used with permission.

## APPENDIX C

### Technology Self-Assessment (Kendall, 1999)

As part of the *Mich-I-Lifts* project you will be picking a technology skill to acquire or improve. In order to proceed, I need to know where you are in your technology skills.

Check the column that best describes your skills today!

| Skill | I can do this with ease. | I can do this. | I can do this with help. | I've heard of this. | What is this? |
|---|---|---|---|---|---|
| **1. Word-process a document** <br> a. write text | | | | | |
| b. cut and paste | | | | | |
| c. insert graphics | | | | | |
| d. create and edit a table | | | | | |
| **2. E-mail** <br> a. send and receive e-mail | | | | | |
| b. send & receive attachments | | | | | |
| c. use a signature file | | | | | |
| d. manage e-mail with filters and folders. | | | | | |

| Skill | I can do this with ease. | I can do this. | I can do this with help. | I've heard of this. | What is this? |
|---|---|---|---|---|---|
| **3. HTML Authoring (Web pages)** | | | | | |
| a.  write text | | | | | |
| b.  cut and paste | | | | | |
| c.  insert graphics | | | | | |
| d.  create and edit a table | | | | | |
| e.  create and edit a link | | | | | |
| f.  author (write) in HTML code | | | | | |
| g.  create a clickable image | | | | | |
| h.  FTP files | | | | | |
| **4. PowerPoint** | | | | | |
| a.  make a slide with text | | | | | |
| b.  make slides containing clip-art | | | | | |
| c.  make a slide with a link to the Web or to another slide | | | | | |
| d.  change the order of the slides | | | | | |
| e.  publish the slide presentation to the Internet | | | | | |
| f.  make a slide with a link to the Web or to another slide | | | | | |
| **5. General PC / Windows Skills** | | | | | |
| a.  use a mouse to open files | | | | | |
| b.  use a mouse to scroll within documents | | | | | |
| c.  save a file | | | | | |
| d.  move a file from one folder to another folder | | | | | |
| e.  create a new folder | | | | | |
| f.  rename a file or folder | | | | | |
| g.  install software | | | | | |
| **6. Digital Camera** | | | | | |
| use a camera and save the pictures to a computer | | | | | |
| **7. Scanner** | | | | | |
| use and save a scanned image to a computer | | | | | |

# 5
# Encouraging Professional Growth: A Statewide Program for Recognizing Foreign Language Teachers

**Stephen Brock**
Omaha (NE) Public Schools

**Vickie Scow**
Nebraska Department of Education

## Introduction

Many factors contribute to the lack of professional development for foreign language educators: apathy, attitude, cost, other obligations, and the lack of substitute teachers, for example. Only one-fourth of foreign language educators belong to any professional language organization. As the profession continues to change, individual teachers must also change; it takes a considerable amount of time and effort to respond to new demands placed on curricula and to adjust to an increasingly diverse student population. Teachers need to discuss their beliefs about language study and to synthesize information provided by recent research in the field.

In an attempt to increase professional development and encourage language educators to participate in professional organizations, the Nebraska Department of Education and the Nebraska Foreign Language Association have instituted the STAR Award–*Study, Travel, Achievement, Recognition*. The award is meant to encourage educators to take responsibility for their own development, and the categories provide a framework for growth as professionals and language leaders. To receive the award, K-16 educators must earn a prescribed number of points given for participation in various development activities within the four categories. Individuals may nominate themselves or be nominated by another person.

In spite of many worthwhile strategies designed to bring about student improvement in the classroom–smaller class sizes, more teacher assistants, programs on student self-esteem–teacher expertise remains the most significant determinant of success, accounting for more than 40% of the gains in overall student performance (Darling-Hammond, 1998). Yet even while the research shows the importance of teacher expertise, many factors mitigate against improved teacher training. Not infrequently, when districts are faced with budget troubles, staff development is among the first programs to be cut. Even if school districts have money for training, many have difficulty locating substitute teachers to allow for teacher training during the school day. Complicating the staff development picture further, teachers themselves have become more reluctant to participate in staff development activities outside of class time, especially if it is at their own expense.

Concurrently, national standards have moved language learning beyond the traditional four skills of listening, speaking, reading, and writing. The *Standards for Foreign Language Learning in the 21ˢᵗ Century* (National Standards in Foreign Language Education Project, 1999) dramatically broaden the scope of foreign language learning beyond its traditional framework of *communication* and *culture*. These new standards also emphasize the use of language to explore transdisciplinary content (*connections*), to examine the very structure between languages and cultures (*comparisons*), and to test newly-learned competencies beyond the setting of the school (*communities*). These five interlocking goals now represent the model for foreign language instruction in all languages across the United States.

**Why the STAR Award?**

Most educators recognize that teaching is a complex activity, and the brief, irregular observations of model classes are not enough to stimulate professional growth. All too often teachers feel isolated and ignored. Danielson (2001, p. 13) maintains that a proper evaluation system "should recognize, develop, and cultivate good teaching." In an attempt to recognize teaching excellence, the creators of the STAR award outlined a schema by which educators can become truly involved in what we think of as "the profession," i.e. the world of memberships, associations, journals, newsletters, conferences, and workshops (Kline, 2000).

The STAR Award places the teacher squarely in charge of personal professional development. In allowing teachers to nominate themselves, the award promotes "self-direction" or "autonomous learners." Cohen (1990) defines "self-directed learning" as a method where "learners make decisions, alone or with the help of others, about what they need or want to know, how they will set objectives for learning, what resources and strategies they will use, and how they will assess their progress" (p. 4).

**What is the STAR Award?**

The STAR Award, a joint effort of the Nebraska Department of Education (NDE) and the Nebraska Foreign Language Association (NFLA), is an annual award presented to second-language educators (K-16) who have "exceeded expectations both within and beyond the classroom" (Scow, 2001, p. 6). Established in 1999, the certificate recognizes a teacher's work within the content area; it also takes into account other clinical experiences, outreach to the community, and the teacher's own work within the professional community (see Appendix A). Winners are recognized at the annual fall NFLA conference, where they receive a certificate signed by the commissioner of NDE. In addition, NDE also mails notice of the honors to local Nebraska newspapers.

To reward more reticent educators, foreign language leaders have approached the award in various ways. For instance, one public school foreign language district supervisor conducted interviews and nominated various teachers within his department. The president of the state's branch of the American Association of Teachers of German (AATG) wrote personal letters to productive German teachers (who had not already nominated themselves) to praise their work and encourage them to apply; consequently, six out of seven possible applicants followed his advice and nominated themselves. Whether nominated by another or by oneself, to attain the award STAR applicants must merit 100 points distributed among the various STAR categories.

In the "S" or "Study" section, teachers receive credit for their most recent graduate degree (in fact, those are the only points that may be carried over from a previous year). In addition, teachers also receive points for pursuing graduate credit in classes at the university, for studying in an international setting, for attending local in-service training, and for mentoring new teachers.

Teachers need to invest time and effort in order to be prepared to deal with the new demands of curricula and an increasingly diverse student population (Jackson, 1996). Teachers need in-service opportunities to develop new skills and attitudes about language learning, to discuss present beliefs about the role of language study, and to synthesize recent information about learning styles, brain development, and language acquisition (Zimmer-Lowe, 2000).

The mentoring component is critical within a discipline already suffering from a teacher shortage because mentoring gives direct and immediate support to the foreign language teacher who is new to the classroom. Berliner states that mentoring during an individual's first five years of teaching has been shown to cut the teacher dropout rate from 50% to 15% (cited in Scherer, 2001, p. 10).

The "Travel" or "T" component of the STAR Award assumes several forms. Teachers are rewarded for visiting sites outside the country and for collecting realia for classroom use. Educators can also glean points for sponsoring student trips abroad or for taking students to statewide foreign language fairs. To attain a more advanced level of language proficiency, the language teacher may use travel as a principal means to hone language skills. Teachers are also rewarded for their participation at statewide, regional, and national workshops and conferences.

In the "A" or "Achievement" category, teachers are credited for honors and awards received through their participation in language organizations at the national, state, and local levels (see Appendix B). In recognition of scholarly activity, ten STAR points are awarded for each presentation at a professional conference, each grant request that is developed, and each article that has been published.

Lastly, the "R" or "Recognition" category credits professional memberships, leadership roles within language organizations, and outreach to the community.

Why does the STAR award recognize and reward professional memberships as such? Of the 100,000 teachers of languages other than English in the United States today, only about one-fourth of them belong to any group whose focus is foreign language education (E. C. Scebold, Personal Communication, 1999)! Connecting teachers with the resources of their professional organizations seems to be a daunting task, however. Apathy, attitude, costs, isolation, other professional obligations–these may be some of the factors limiting an individual's participation. Whatever the case, professional groups in which the great majority of potential members have no communication with one another can hardly be viewed as being productive and progressive, or even professional, for that matter. The STAR Award is one vehicle where participation, especially active participation through leadership positions, rewards the language teacher. The award may thus act as an external stimulus to develop and "grow" language leaders within the state.

As the award originates in part from an NFLA initiative, applicants are rewarded for their work within that organization especially: mere attendance at the NFLA Conference merits 20 points, as does professional membership within NFLA. An ACTFL membership earns an applicant 10 points, while all other language memberships earn only 5 points.

## Conclusion

Teachers of languages need to take advantage of the many professional development opportunities available to them. Nebraska's STAR Award is one way to recognize professionals who devote time to improving their knowledge and skills and who become involved in professional networking. We face a critical time in the study of international languages in the United States. Though the demand upon second-language educators has never been greater, failure to produce students with proficiency may thwart all our efforts. The STAR Award is one way to recognize those teachers who are already outstanding and productive. To those who are less active and in need of more professional development, the award provides a framework of ideas that will enable them to succeed as educators and to grow as professionals.

## References

Cohen, A. D. (1990). *Language learning: Insights for learners, teachers, and researchers*. New York: Newbury House.
Darling-Hammond, L. (1998). *Handbook on research on teacher education*. New York: Association of Teacher Educators.
Danielson, C. (2001). New trends in teacher evaluation. *Educational Leadership, 58* (5), 12-15.

Jackson, C. W. (1996). National standards and the challenge of articulation. In B.H. Wing (Ed.), *Foreign languages for all: Challenges and choices* (pp. 115-139). Lincolnwood, IL: National Textbook Company.

Kline, R. R. (2000). *New visions architecture of the profession issues paper.* Ames, IA: National K-12 Foreign Language Resource Center.

National Standards in Foreign Language Education Project (1999). *Standards for foreign language learning in the 21st century.* Lawrence, KS: Allen Press.

Scherer, M. (2001). ). Improving the quality of the teaching force. A conversation with David Berliner. *Educational Leadership, 58* (8), 6-8.

Scow, V. (2001). Star awards. *Vision and Views, 1* (3), 6-7.

Zimmer-Lowe, H. (2000). Professional development and change in foreign language education. In R. M. Terry (Ed.), *Agents of change in a changing age* (pp. 169-209). Lincolnwood, IL: National Textbook Company.

**Appendix A**

**STAR Award**

Nebraska foreign language teachers exceed expectations both within and beyond the classroom. The Nebraska Department of Education and the Nebraska Foreign Language Association want you to know your efforts are not going unnoticed! You exemplify superior qualities with your dedication to students, outreach to the community, and continual efforts for improvement. We want to recognize you for excellence in foreign language education with the third annual STAR AWARDS for Nebraska foreign language teachers. All honorees will be recognized at the Nebraska Foreign Language Association Fall Conference.

In order to apply for the award three conditions must be met: (1) You must be a current foreign language educator in a Nebraska elementary, junior high/middle school, secondary, postsecondary, or four-year institution. (2) You must be an NFLA member. (3) You must be able to compile 100 points on the application form. All presentations, association offices held, conference attendance, etc. must have taken place between May 1, 2001 and April 30, 2002. For example, if you held an association office from October 2000 to October 2001 or if you took office October 2001, it counts. The only points that reflect credit from previous years are the *Most Recent Graduate Degree* points. Please attach a second page, if additional lines are needed.

If you wish to apply, please complete the application form and send it Foreign Language Education, Nebraska Department of Education, PO Box 94987, Lincoln, NE 68509.

**Appendix B**

**STAR Award Criteria**

### Nebraska Foreign Language STAR Awards

Name _____

Home Address_____

Home Phone_____

- Include activities from: May 1, 2001 to April 30, 2002

- Attach an additional page if additional lines are needed.

- Mail by May 1, 2002 to: Vickie Scow
  Foreign Language Ed.
  NE Dept. of Education
  PO Box 94987
  Lincoln, NE 68509

**STUDY**

**Most Recent Graduate Degree**

| | | | |
|---|---|---|---|
| ____Bachelor's | (5) | ____Master's | (10) |
| ____Doctorate | (15) | ____Other | (10) |

**Graduate Credits**
(Earned during current year; 1 pt. per credit hour) ____Total Credits
List place/classes:




**International Study**
(Earned during current year; 1 pt. per credit hour) ____Total Credits
List place/classes:




**Inservice**
____Local District (1 pt. half-day/2 pt. full day)
____ESU Foreign Language Workshop   (5)
____Other (s):                          (5)

**Teachers Mentoring Teachers**
____Student Teacher   (10)   Student's Name_____
____Teacher Mentor   (10)   Teacher's Name_____

**TRAVEL**

**International Travel**
_____Place(s) Visited:    (10)

_____Collected Realia for Classroom Use    (10)

_____ Sponsored Student Travel Group       (20)
    Where:                                         When:                            How Many:

**Conferences**
_____ACTFL          (5 pts/day)          _____Central States    (5 pts/day)
_____NFLA           (20)                 _____AATF/G/SP         (5 pts/day)
_____NETA           (10)                 _____Other(s):    (10)

**Foreign Language Fair**
_____Where attended: _____ (5)      _____# of students:

**Foreign Language Related Performances/Field Trips**
_____Where attended: _____ (5)      _____ # of students:


**ACHIEVEMENT**

**Awards/Honors (National, State, Local)**

_____ (10)

_____ (10)

_____ (10)

**Presentations**

_____ (10)
Place:                                         Date:

_____ (10)
Place:                                         Date:

**Published State Articles**

_____ (10)
Source:                                        Date:

**Published National Articles**

_____ (10)
Source:                                        Date:

**Grants Awarded**

_____    (10)

**RECOGNITION OF PROFESSIONALISM**

**Professional Membership**

| | | | | | |
|---|---|---|---|---|---|
| _____ACTFL | (10) | | _____TESOL | (5) | |
| _____NFLA | (20) | | _____ MLA | (5) | |
| _____AATF | (5) | | _____NEA/NSEA/LEA | (5) | |
| _____NATF | (5) | | _____ Phi Delta Kappa | (5) | |
| _____AATG | (5) | | _____ Other (s): | | |
| _____NATG | (5) | | _____ | (5) | |
| _____AATSP | (5) | | _____ | (5) | |
| _____NATSP | (5) | | _____ | (5) | |

**Identify Association Offices Held**

_____    (10)
_____    (10)
_____    (10)
_____    (10)

**Leadership**

_____FL Club Sponsor    (10)
_____Listserve    (5)
_____Other (s):    (5)

**Outreach/Community Service**

_____Exch. Student Host    (10)
_____Interpreter    (1 pt. per hour)
_____FL-Related Volunteer    (10)
_____FL-Related Professional Organization    (10)
_____Other(s):    (10)

**TOTALS:**

| | |
|---|---|
| Study | _____ |
| Travel | _____ |
| Achievement | _____ |
| Recognition of Professionalism | _____ |

**TOTAL:**    _____

# 6
# Language Acquisition, Culture Acquisition, Literature Acquisition: An Integrated Textual Approach to Beginning and Intermediate Classes

**Douglas K. Benson**
Kansas State University

Recent articles by Shanahan (1997) and Kramsch & Kramsch (2000) frame in important ways two questions posed for decades by department heads and language faculty: What should be the points of articulation between lower-level language classes, where communicative competence is clearly the goal, and the study of cultural and literary texts with their broader humanistic concerns? What should be the instructor's role in "bridging the gap" between language and literature? Both articles point out four crucial elements in this debate:

(1) Foreign language learning in the U. S. has become widely accepted for its utilitarian and career-oriented benefits.
(2) In recent years, the enhanced environment for language learning does not reflect a broad and equally enhanced appreciation of the importance of liberal education.
(3) Data-based (mostly ESL) research in applied linguistics and second language acquisition has given us remarkable advances but has largely ignored the cultural and literary text as a unique vehicle for language acquisition.
(4) Researchers in the field of language acquisition have been reluctant to utilize cultural and literary texts because their findings are derived more from intuition than from logic and are therefore not scientifically verifiable.

The above-mentioned elements highlight problems in utilizing cultural and literary texts in the language class. Yet as Shanahan (1997) notes, all who work in the field of culture and literature and also in language acquisition know that these texts provide human-interest data that energize learning. They also provide access to a cultural perspective that Williams et al. (1994) described as the *"informing spirit* of a whole way of life," a vehicle for learners to create Kramsch's "third places" between L1/C1 and L2/C2.[1] Literary texts introduce and frame the cultural elements that bring meaning to and energize all language in its real-world uses. These texts have a decided effect on the development of communicative competence. Mythic, symbolic, and metaphorical expressions permeate every aspect of our lives and those of our students. Cultures are constantly evolving and producing multiple meanings for linguistic elements. Cultural and literary texts then offer us the raw material to "recalibrate" our reading instruments and to penetrate the complex discourse strategies of cultures. At the same time, we need to broaden our notion of "text" to include film, television, advertising, and music, and to study their effects on language learning. Shanahan challenges us to think not only of the "affective filter," the barrier to acquisition, but also of the "affective magnet," the positive elements of affect in motivating students to learn language. Finally, he notes that the same analytical skills that inform literary study and language acquisition research can be applied to "intuitive forms of knowledge" as well (pp. 166-171).

This is an exciting time to be teaching language, largely because of the results that we see from the recent findings of acquisition research. Shanahan (1997) describes the gaping hole in our pedagogical arsenal and the "great divide" between specialists in language acquisition and those in culture and literature, and he presents us with many challenges. It is time to re-examine these same issues raised a decade ago by Swaffar, Arens, and Byrnes (1991), Galloway (1992), and Kramsch (1993), and to raise new ones that can perhaps focus on teaching and research of the type that Shanahan recommends. It is time to highlight the parallels and points of commonality in teaching language, culture, and literature and to suggest additional strategies that can move our students along. Two of these issues form the base around which the rest may be clustered: How can we mitigate the lack of articulation between lower-level language classes and the study of literature? How can we fit cultural and literary texts into a program that is based on the communicative approach?

## Literature, Culture, and the Beginning Language Course

Shanahan (1997) repeats an assumption of our profession that is rarely seen refuted: students in the very first course of basic language study, because of their linguistic limitations, are not equipped to handle cultural and literary texts. Teachers must somehow adapt these texts for the learners' consumption. Swaffar et al. (1991) recommend early intervention in the training of general reading strategies and suggest expository "gist" readings of familiar text types in beginning classes to force "top-down" strategies, balancing the word-for-word "bottom-up" style that is too often the sole focus of classroom reading. Their suggestions for presenting cultural and literary texts, however, are targeted principally at upper-intermediate and advanced adult learners.

According to Shanahan (1997), "not all literature is accessible to all learners at all proficiency levels," and instructors often surrender to the inevitable and do not even include literature (p. 171). When the literary text is taught, the class is usually a lecture format (sometimes, in desperation, even in English!) rather than an interactive format involving the students. Alternatively, one may resort to the ubiquitous "comprehension questions," but they contribute little or nothing to the language learning experience. Rosenblatt (1938/1995) insists that we also must get past the idea that literary texts are somehow autonomous entities that can be objectively analyzed.

A personal anecdote will illustrate the point: Some ten years ago I visited a junior-high beginning Spanish class as part of the first of our two year-long NEH institutes for rural secondary language teachers. I had brought along a few of Bécquer's briefest love poems (*Rimas*) to demonstrate how poetry would sound in the learners' new language. The first was his *XXI*, "*¿Qué es poesía?*" (What is Poetry?), with its oft-recited question and response: "*Poesía eres tú*" (Poetry... is you). We talked a bit about the conventions of Romantic love poetry, not an easy thing to do with a class in the full bloom of puberty onset. One young man, clearly frustrated, finally summoned up the courage of his thirteen years to ask, in English: "Why is it romantic? Why can't it be a grandmother answering her grandson? Maybe he just came home from school and his grandmother is thinking what the poem 'says.'" I sat there stunned as I re-read the poem in search of evidence to the contrary. There was none. I had just been trumped by a seventh-grader.

All too often we believe that beginning learners, because they are at rudimentary communicative stages in their language development, cannot learn to analyze and interpret cultural and literary texts, especially since they are likely unaware of the writer's life and cultural circumstances. The fact remains, however, that even young beginners can utilize a wealth of life experience and a knowledge of discourse types, situations, and reading strategies to draw inferences from such texts. This process can be enhanced if the students are provided a model and structures within which to work, especially in group-learning environments that lessen their inhibitions and heighten the affective dimension of their learning experience. In too many classrooms, learners are never permitted to speak to each other or to the teacher except in formulaic ways. Individuals must "do their own work," and negotiating the meanings of cultural and literary material is not welcomed.

We also must recognize the "blinders" that our own formal literary preparation has created for us. We are often so convinced of the need to present our one "correct" textual reading based on extensive research about the writer that we are unable to see other possibilities that a text may offer. This practice contradicts one contemporary view, expressed often by the French critic Paul Ricoeur, that sees the literary text as totally dislocated from the particular circumstances of the writer. One can read for meaning as opposed to doing historical, critical analysis. Ellis (1974), among many others, views this absence of pragmatic applicability as fundamental to the reading experience: "Literary texts are defined as those that are used by the society in such a way that *the text is not taken as specifically relevant to the immediate context of its origin*" (pp. 43-44). It is precisely this use that frees a text and gives it literary immortality.

Certainly we want our upper-level and graduate students to be well versed in the socio-historical context of the writer and the text as well as in theories of literary criticism. In the first few language courses, however, a focus on these aspects prior to (or as a substitute for) helping learners discover what texts mean often gets in the way of open, imaginative reading and the simultaneous language learning that develops along with it. Learner analysis and interpretation must come first. Any "background" comes only when learners are ready for it. We can begin immediately the process of using texts to help students see themselves and the world, including their new language and culture, by reconstructing the text's context through "cultural readings" (Galloway, 1992; Swaffar, 1992) and "teaching language along the cultural faultline" (Kramsch, 1993, pp. 205-232). This allows for the comparing and contrasting of corresponding elements in the student's own culture and the one being studied.[2]

The acknowledgment that the reader is just as important as the text under-scores the need to study the implicit underlying cultural and social assumptions of any work, an enterprise that allows readers to "make these the basis for scrutiniz-ing their own assumptions" (Rosenblatt, 1938/1995, pp. 289-295). Doing so, in turn, will lead the students to consider the extent to which they themselves fit or do not fit the norms of their own culture. Ideally, it will lead them to want to study more about the circumstances of the production of the text and its cultural system. We must also go beyond the presentation of cultural material as mere factual in-formation and delve into the complex interrelationships that actually determine cultural contexts: "Cultural differences must be discovered as dialogic practices, not learned as monologic features" (Swaffar, 1992, p. 238).

The teacher should strive to create an introspective and collaborative envi-ronment in which students are encouraged to analyze and interpret (1) the text and its structures, (2) the strategies and techniques utilized by the writers, and (3) the perspectives dramatized through the work's narrators and other characters. If these elements are not provided, we should not expect students suddenly to be able to begin this type of analysis during the fourth semester of study. Language acquisi-tion, culture acquisition, and literature acquisition are developmental processes that take time and careful nurturing. Kramsch (1993) explains:

> ...the meaning of cross-cultural encounters is hardly or barely realized at the time. Rather, it appears at various levels of under-standing at a much later date, from personal reflection and repeated attempts to bring together for oneself the various pieces of the cultural puzzle, and compare its emerging picture with that of others. (p. 232)

It is time to think again about language learning as an integrated enterprise. Recent findings in language acquisition already suggest an appropriate classroom format in which to conduct this effort, even though most current research does not address cultural and literary texts specifically. In student-centered "communicative" classrooms the following elements are present: (1) learners are interpreting, negotiating, and expressing meanings among themselves by means of the target language; (2) the importance of the social dimension is emphasized; (3) and the development of higher-level cognitive skills is encouraged.

As Savignon (1972) demonstrated more than 25 years ago and as Byrnes (1998) reaffirms today, purely grammatical activities, disconnected from meaning and context, may inhibit rather than foment the progress of our students in their ability to interpret and express themselves. If learners never have the opportunity to negotiate conversational meanings and to circumlocute unknown vocabulary, as in the real world, they will carry a dictionary around as if that were a normal communicative strategy (Berry-Bravo, 1993). Current research demonstrates that if students learn about the world and about themselves *through* the new language, they learn more quickly, remember more, and do not panic the first time a real native speaker addresses them. Instead of speaking to learn grammatical forms, they speak to learn about each other and the world. Instead of learning to read, they read to learn with a fixed purpose in their minds (Knutson, 1997; Kramsch, 1993). Instead of writing grammatical forms, they write for the same reasons as those of us in the real world do: to communicate meanings with a real person and to carry out pragmatic goals. To paraphrase von Humboldt, we cannot teach a language, we can only create the conditions for its acquisition (cited in Lee & VanPatten, 1995, p. 22).

We know, in addition, that language teaching can be more effective if we think of the linguistic formation of our students as a gradual process that has steps and stages. Almost all the current literature about second-language reading underscores the need for preparatory activities (pre-reading), a thorough cycle of minimal, re-entry processing tasks during the lesson (reading), and activities for assimilation and application to the world outside the text afterwards (post-reading). Corresponding sequences are widely recommended for aural comprehension, oral production, writing, and culture study. Typical preparatory activities take the form of "schema activation," i.e., the use of learners' previous knowledge of the world, the language, the discourse forms, and the strategies that each culture uses to communicate. In this way learners can be taught to read or listen by encoding meaning instead of just decoding forms. They will be able to skim for the general topic, scan for specific information, guess at the meaning of words and forms, "chunk" related information for memory storage, and take notes for discussion. As part of the process, they will come to realize that they may never understand all the words, but that they can be confident of their ability to understand a text. The *post-reading* (synthesis) stage links previous knowledge with the text's information and language forms, encouraging both a new perspective and a way of expressing it in the new language.

In answer to our protests that beginners cannot understand language well enough to produce their own meanings, Lee and VanPatten (1995) point out that we ourselves regularly use "comprehensible input" with our own children who understand and produce large quantities of language. Our children learn by using the same system of hypothesis and verification that adult learners use to process any new information. Beginning language learners are no different. If we provide appropriate structures and patterns, they can understand language that we have never "taught" them and that they have never heard before. We can both enhance and accelerate the natural process of language learning, but we cannot change the sequence of natural acquisition orders, individual learning styles, nor individual rates of learning. Traditional grammatical formats do not address these issues.

If the teacher approaches cultural and literary texts only through lecture standard comprehension checks, learners' acquisition mechanisms shut down. Comprehension questions and other fact-based forms of evaluation do not activate problem-solving strategies (Swaffar et al., 1991). We all know the glazed eyes that respond to lectures and the "look back and lift off" strategies that students use for comprehension questions. If learners do not have the opportunity to interpret, negotiate, and express meanings, their progress in learning how to do it by themselves will be slow or null (as true for graduate students as for beginners). Byrnes (1998) notes that language accuracy is not the only issue here. Swaffar et al. (1991) concur: "*L2 reading comprehension is a function of cognitive development, the ability to think within the framework of the second language*" (p. 63). Thus, we cannot expect that language instruction by itself will somehow automatically prepare students to read cultural and literary texts later on. In fact, "an exclusive language focus in beginning instruction sabotages interactive reading.... Students need to realize that knowing a language and reading in a second language are complementary but distinctly different abilities" (p. 32). The teaching of facts must be replaced by students' learning of multiple relationships. We must begin to think in terms of educational rather than merely instructional objectives (Kramsch, 1993) and of affective over purely linguistic outcomes (Lalande, 1988).

## Literature, Culture, and Language: A Dialogical Relationship

Instead of presenting a personal interpretation of the cultural or literary text in lecture format, the teacher needs to provide students with the opportunity and the strategies to analyze and interpret the text first. Only then will they begin to arrive at the multiple possibilities that any text offers. Other interpretations must be encouraged and recognized as long as students can show us the "evidence" in the text itself. A "wrap-up" class discussion and follow-up by the teacher will then be more enthusiastically received and often can focus in general discussion on those points not brought out. In short, as Bretz and Persin (1987) point out, the classroom need not be a place of mystery where learners are expected to divine how the teacher arrived at an interpretation. Instead, the class can be a place of discovery for everyone, including the teacher.

The general theory of reading as interaction between text and reader, summarized by Lee and VanPatten (1995), applies to cultural and literary texts in a special way. If the reader does not participate, there can be no aesthetic experience. Any text is a "blueprint," a plan for reading and not the reading itself (pp. 189-199). Iser's theory (1974) supposes that literary and cultural texts are not finished products nor physical objects but temporal sequences of open-ended stimuli waiting to guide and to be opened up and completed by their readers. The best texts contain naturally-occurring "gaps," the world and cultural vision of the writer differing from the world, experiences, and expectations of the reader. In literature such "gaps" are intentional, part of any good text, distinguishing them from locutionary types of writing such as newspapers and telegrams. Rosenblatt (1938/1995) sees this difference in terms of the purely public aspects of meaning in nonliterary reading as opposed to a combination of public and private meanings in the "aesthetic stance" that readers must adopt to make a text literary. Both she and Kramsch (1993) point out that all texts exist on a continuum between the two poles. Any text can be literary if a reader addresses it as such, and even very literary texts are too often used in language classrooms as mere sources of facts and information (Rosenblatt, pp. 292-293; Kramsch, pp. 124, 131-134).

In cultural texts the "gaps" come from differing expectations and forms of responding to universal values and life experiences, thus affording students the opportunity to work in groups, exchange experiences, and use their cognitive abilities. They already have different experiences in their own culture, and they know different information. This situation corresponds perfectly to classic "information-gap" group-learning activities in which each participant has information that the others do not have. Students must work together to achieve a consensus.

A considerable amount of research and discussion during the last two decades has focused on the teaching of culture and literature in language classes, for personal as well as linguistic development.[3] However, as Bretz and Persin noted in 1987, few universities teach us to teach literature, a situation that is changing only very slowly. Research on the use of cultural and literary texts at the beginning levels of foreign language learning is almost nonexistent (Shook, 1996, 1997). Yet, once again one hears urgent, substantive calls for an integrated approach at both the secondary and university levels, in part as a response to the new foreign language Standards. Byrnes puts her view of a university foreign language sequence succinctly: "literature from the beginning, language through the end" (cited in Phillips & Terry, 1999, p. 6).

Culture and literature are not a part of language, though from our narrow perspective as language professionals they may seem so. Rather, language and literature are parts of a culture and of a larger context as well. They are means to an end, not the end itself. A language and a text that are neither heard nor read and that are not pressed into the service of learning about the world and oneself produce empty academic exercises and mindless memorization. As Davis (1989) and Stoll (1992) assert, literary language and situations are not isolated phenomena;

rather, they are representative of the human community, necessarily derived from what we know. Literary and cultural texts allow learners to get beyond their self-protective "shields," to have vicarious experiences of great diversity, to "rehearse" situations that have and have not yet occurred in their own lives, and to develop an imagination for understanding and controlling their own emotional reactions in real life (Rosenblatt, 1938/1995, pp. 175-216). These texts allow language professionals to achieve more compelling effects by teaching to the affective rather than purely to the cognitive realm.

### Activities Toward the Study of Literary and Cultural Texts

The proficiency movement provides much of what is necessary to help students learn to process cultural and literary texts from the first weeks of the beginning class. The American Council on the Teaching of Foreign Languages (ACTFL) proficiency descriptors for the Novice-level focus on lists or categories of words, memorized formulaic speech, and the ability to answer choice and yes-no questions. Using a family tree as the basis, Lee and VanPatten (1995) demonstrate how to use simple, cultural information to tell a "story" ("comprehensible input") in the first few days of Spanish 1 (pp. 46-47). The ACTFL Novice-level descriptors closely match the input style they model. Beginning learners discover how to describe their own families to each other in simple terms ("information exchange"). This type of narrative input and output can be used as a model and then expanded when we ask learners to generate a family tree of some well-known fairy tale or other popular cultural text. The activity thus links the personal and concrete to more universal and abstract concepts while appealing to the affective dimension of learning. (Consider the number of fairy tales in which a biological parent is missing.) As the class progresses, naturally-occurring vocabulary groups such as numbers, colors, dates, and seasons can be linked to L1 and L2 cultural and literary situations (e.g., movies and television, popular songs, children's rhymes and stories, short poems) as well as to the personal experiences of the teacher and the learners.

The ACTFL Intermediate-level learners can describe people, places, objects, and situations in simple sentences; ask questions; role play everyday situations; and handle concrete "survival" topics. To make the transition from Novice to Intermediate, students can work in groups with more extended poems and stories to describe speakers and narrators, characters, motivations, situations, and time and place (see Appendix). If a text does not provide certain information, it offers learners the perfect opportunity to make it up. The imagined text is just as valuable for language learning and for psychological and social development as the one on the page.

The *pre-reading* phase so widely recommended will not work, however, if learners prepare to read a text only by studying a list of relevant vocabulary. For example, if the text is the short story "The Old Piano" by the Venezuelan Rómulo

Gallegos, the students can be misled in their attempt to evaluate the target culture by comparing the fictional family to their own. One must work in both directions: "...we must be ever cognizant of the learners' need for security, support, and validation of both their C1 topical coordinates and the status of their L2/C2 knowledge under construction" (Galloway, 1992, p. 101). One has to prepare the way first, perhaps weeks earlier, through a comparison of the family systems of Anglo-Americans and Spaniards or Hispanic Americans, taking special care to avoid stereotypes. The focus could be, for example, the complex ways in which *both* family systems have created traditional and modern forms as they respond to present-day changes. Shook (1997) demonstrates a range of techniques for working with student schemata when texts come from other cultures.

We can now visualize a way to unite many different facets of the class into a single strategic and thematic learning experience. The Spanish class that studies the "to be" verbs *ser* and *estar* first by means of comprehensible input and then by explicit, structured, grammatical input (Lee & VanPatten, 1995)[4] will later use the same grammar and vocabulary in circumlocution activities such as those outlined by Berry-Bravo (1993) ("It's a person who.../an object that... /a place where..."). Finally, following the model of Swaffar, Arens, and Byrnes (1991), these steps can be applied in a learner-centered analysis and interpretation of a simple literary text (p. 120). A class module on the family or on ecology can draw upon many different texts: topic-related, personal teacher narratives, taped interviews with native speakers, videos, cultural articles from periodicals, or literature. Students use their notes on all the texts as input for their growing database of information and opinion on the subject. A text may serve simultaneously as comprehensible input on a given topic, as structured input for a particular grammatical structure, as a writer's particular "take" on the topic that can be compared to a learner's experience, and as a vehicle for improving skills in analysis, interpretation, and evaluation. This type of text-based "problem-solving" approach, whether applied to grammar, vocabulary, personal experience, or cultural and literary "detective work," serves many purposes. At the same time, it combines a range of cognitive skills and learning styles with the impact of affective motivation.

In an integrated approach there are fewer limitations on the sequencing of materials. We need not follow exactly or even use a standard language textbook. A cultural or literary text can provide "first contact" with a new topic; it can be the central activity for a topic; or it can serve as a "wrap-up" or evaluative activity that leads to a specific product (e.g., a composition that outlines and documents the learner's opinion, a chart or cognitive map, a letter to a text's character, a group role play, or a "reader's theater"). If the modular sequence is thought out beforehand, the post-reading activity for one text serves seamlessly as the pre-reading activity for the next. Points of comparison and contrast among texts and personal experiences can provide the material for final evaluation of the learners' ability to handle that topic in its linguistic, cultural, and literary forms.

**Challenges and Goals**

Three possible pitfalls remain to be discussed: (1) Each text offers many interpretations, but it also rejects many. One college student tried to read Bécquer's poem "*¿Qué es poesía?*" as an expression of the Spanish socio-political situation. Another saw the speaker as a high-school literature teacher conversing with a student. As the 7th-grader demonstrated, the poem suggests many possible situations: romantic love, family love, speakers and characters of a variety of genders and ages. However, there are situations in which language is culturally incongruent. (2) The teacher-centered "Atlas complex" that Lee and VanPatten (1995) mention is alive and well in language classrooms, at the beginning as well as advanced levels. One has to be willing to concede that the ultimate authority resides in the text, not in the teacher nor in the student. We learners (teachers as well as students) need to become critical of our own first impulses and cognizant of what Galloway (1992, p.111) calls the "fallibility of assumption." "Encouraging good thinking strategies will mean allowing students to be 'wrong' so they can discover for themselves why they are wrong, or not totally right" (p. 113). If the text allows a reading, the reading is acceptable. If not, it cannot be forced. (3) Once students have "ownership" of the text, they remember it better and they are invariably more interested in biographical and historical information. More importantly, they do not attempt to impose the narrow limitations of a writer's life on the texts. Often a biographical interpretation provides a perfectly credible reading, but only one of many. Focusing only on the biographical can also lead learners to believe that the text's narrator is the writer, an assumption that is unfounded and even harmful, particularly in the study of literature (Ellis, 1974, pp. 113-115).

The Appendix includes a list of possible literary analysis strategies, starting with those appropriate for beginning learners and proceeding in complexity as students develop in their ability to analyze and interpret texts. The questions that exemplify each category are not "comprehension questions" because there is no single "correct" answer that the teacher already knows; rather, they are approaches to literary (and often cultural) texts that provide a structure in which learners can produce a variety of real-world meanings through language. As learners progress they should be able to handle most of the list, an accomplishment that in turn means the transition to literature and civilization classes will be more productive and enjoyable for both learners and teachers.

There are many other approaches and activities for processing cultural and literary texts, but the tendency to present such material in classes only on "culture Fridays" or to reduce cultural and literary texts to mere sources of factual data must be resisted. Nor should one *supplant* language learning with culture and literary study. They should all be integrated.

Finally, if meaning-based activities have been stressed during the development phase, meaning-based evaluation will be necessary as well. Discrete-point grammar tests only occasionally serve any purpose. Evaluation tasks should be scored globally: How are the ideas presented? Is the work related to the tasks in the class? How is it evaluated? Does it represent an appropriate awareness of Kramsch's (1993) "cultural faultline"? Would a native speaker understand the language, even if it is not perfect, or would it be incomprehensible? How does the student *communicate* knowledge at this level? Is there evidence of progress?

Returning to the challenges presented by Shanahan (1997) and Kramsch and Kramsch (2000), it seems the issue is not to defend *whether* to include cultural and literary texts but *how* to do it and *when* to start. At the beginning level, often the focus is "covering the book," and one does not realize that many exercises and texts from standard textbooks can be adapted to an integrated approach or replaced with others that produce better results. When textbooks contain few global, "affective magnet" activities, these must be invented, opening up new ways to broaden and enrich classroom activities, to make them more productive and culturally relevant, and to insert them deliberately into an integrated, coherent language curriculum.

Quantitative and qualitative acquisition research can focus on how the use of texts in these and similar ways enhances progress in the language as well as enriches the cognitive, affective, and social dimensions of our learners' awareness. Pedagogical change, like cultural change, comes slowly. The old "class struggle" between "literature for the elite" and "language as democratic enterprise" need not frustrate us throughout the next century:

> Are teachers ready to examine their own cultural premises, reveal their opinions and their own interpretations of texts, and engage in double-voiced discourse with their students? [....] What often constrains teachers is the fear of the imagination, of unexplainable and uncontrollable meanings, of paradox and ambiguity. If they listen to and explore further what their students are saying through their ill-formed utterances, their silences, their non-verbal language, they will discover where the forces of change are and where teachers can, as the saying goes, 'make a difference' (Kramsch, 1993, p. 93).

Separating *language* from *content* deprives "both language and content classes of the unique quality that justifies their presence [...] in the first place" (Byrnes, 1998, p. 270). The language we teach is a means, not a goal, but it is a powerful center around which we can "circle the wagons" (Kramsch, 1993, p. 36). Students who study language with no compelling cognitive, affective, and social *content* or who study *content* with little opportunity to process it personally through new language skills are losing both ways. Those who have no opportunity to use the communicative and analytical skills that can develop in foreign language classes are missing their potential to become self-directed thinkers–that is, to train for their lives.

**Notes**

[1]    Kramsch (1993) explains "looking for Third Places" as a way of giving students the power to act upon and utilize fully their learning environment. Learners are not just passive consumers of educational materials. They create meaning as they negotiate their way through cultural and literary texts. As a result, they discover and begin to create neutral "third places" between the native and target languages, cultures, and literatures.

[2]    Kramsch (1993) advocates teaching in ways that constantly emphasize the points of convergence and divergence between the native and target cultures, and between the individual and culture-wide views of things:

> ... the universals can get their proper meaning (or weighting) only from the particular voice of the writer and the particular voice can be listened to and understood only through the universal. What we need is to view the two irreducible perspectives in a dialogic relationship that respects their contradictory nature and hopes for a personal resolution through dialogue (p. 226).

She accurately points out that textual authenticity may not be the central issue. We must consider as well the authentic *usage* of texts and learning behaviors in different educational traditions as we help learners to read the "codes" that produce the texts, "in a constant tension between native and target culture." Authentic texts are of questionable use if teachers accept uncritically the dominant educational culture of their society and present such texts uncritically as "authentic" for all target-culture members.

[3]    Especially notable is the pioneering work of Arens, Byrnes, Galloway, Kramsch, Swaffar, and Rosenblatt. Of great help as well are articles or chapters on specific aspects such as those, by no means exhaustive, listed in the "Works cited" and "Suggested readings" of this article.

[4]    Lee and VanPatten (1995) present a compelling alternative model of *explicit* grammatical instruction based on: (1) contextualized grammar and vocabulary in the form of global "comprehensible input" on a topic; (2) related "structured input" activities that keep meaning in focus but handle only one grammatical form at a time; (3) meaning-based, "structured output" activities that also handle only one form at a time, all the time heading toward (4) "information exchange" activities that focus exclusively on information and use a variety of grammatical forms and vocabulary already learned. Their research indicates that learners who receive this type of explicit, meaning-based, grammatical instruction in context not only understand better, but they also produce language structures at the same level as, or better than, those who work only with traditional, "form-focused" grammatical exercises.

# References

Berry-Bravo, J. (1993). Teaching the art of circumlocution. *Hispania, 76*, 371-377.

Bretz, M. L., & Persin, M. (1987). The application of critical theory to literature at the introductory level: A working model for teacher preparation. *The Modern Language Journal, 71*, 165-170.

Byrnes, H. (Ed.). (1998). *Learning foreign and second languages: Perspectives in research and scholarship*. New York: Modern Language Association.

Davis, J. N. (1989). The act of reading in the foreign language: Pedagogical implications of Iser's reader-response theory. *The Modern Language Journal, 73*, 420-428.

Ellis, J. M. (1974). *The theory of literary criticism: A logical analysis*. Berkeley: University of California Press.

Galloway, V. (1992). Toward a cultural reading of authentic texts. In H. Byrnes (Ed.), *Languages for a multicultural world in transition* (pp. 87-121). Lincolnwood, IL: National Textbook Co.

Iser, W. (1974). The reading process: A phenomenological approach. In W. Iser (Ed.), *The implied reader: Patterns of communication in prose fiction from Bunyan to Beckett* (pp. 274-294). Baltimore: Johns Hopkins University Press.

Knutson, E. M. (1997). Reading with a purpose: Communicative reading tasks for the foreign language classroom. *Foreign Language Annals, 30*, 49-57.

Kramsch, C. (1993). *Context and culture in language teaching*. Oxford: Oxford University Press.

Kramsch, C., & Kramsch, O. (2000). The avatars of literature in language study. *The Modern Language Journal, 84*, 553-573.

LaLande, J. F. (1988). Teaching literature and culture in the high school foreign language class. *Foreign Language Annals, 21*, 573-581.

Lee, J. F., & VanPatten, B. (1995). *Making communicative language teaching happen*. New York: McGraw-Hill.

Phillips. J. K., and Terry, R. M. (Eds.). (1999). *Foreign language standards: Linking research, theories, and practices*. Lincolnwood, IL: National Textbook Co.

Rosenblatt, L. M. (1938/1995). *Literature as exploration* (5th ed.). New York: Modern Language Association.

Savignon, S. J. (1972). *Communicative competence: An experiment in foreign language teaching*. Philadelphia: Center for Curriculum Development.

Shanahan, D. J. (1997). Articulating the relationship between language, literature, and culture: Toward a new agenda for foreign language teaching and research. *The Modern Language Journal, 81*, 164-174.

Shook, D. J. (1996). Foreign language literature and the beginning learner-reader. *Foreign Language Annals, 29*, 201-216.

Shook, D. J. (1997). Identifying and overcoming possible mismatches in the beginning reader–literary text interaction. *Hispania, 80*, 234-243.

Stoll, A. K. (1992). Teaching Golden Age drama: Metatheater as organizing principle. *Hispania, 75*, 1343-1347.

Swaffar, J. K., Arens, K., & Byrnes, H. (1991). *Reading for meaning: An integrated approach to language learning.* Englewood Cliffs, NJ: Prentice Hall.

Swaffar, J. K. (1992). Written texts and cultural readings. In C. Kramsch & S. McConnell-Ginet (Eds), *Text and context: Cross-cultural perspectives on language study* (pp. 238-250). Lexington, MA: D. C. Heath.

Williams, M., Lively, M., & Harper, J. (1994). Higher order thinking skills: Tools for bridging the gap. *Foreign Language Annals, 27*, 405-426.

**Suggested Readings**

Arries, J. F. (1994). Constructing culture study units: A blueprint and practical tools. *Foreign Language Annals, 27*, 523-534.

Bakhtin, M. M. (1981). *The dialogic imagination: Four essays.* Austin: University of Texas Press.

Ballman, T. L. (1996). Integrating vocabulary, grammar and culture: A model five-day communicative lesson plan. *Foreign Language Annals, 29*, 37-44.

Ballman, T. L. (1997). Enhancing beginning language courses through content-enriched instruction. *Foreign Language Annals, 30*, 175-186.

Barnett, M. (1992). Writing as a process. *Northeast Conference Newsletter, 31*, 16-19, 51-55.

Benson, D. K. (2001). Language acquisition, culture acquisition, literature acquisition: An integrated approach to language learning. *Kansas Foreign Language Association Bulletin, Spring*, 15-21.

Blake, R. J. (1998). The role of technology in second language learning. In H. Byrnes (Ed.), *Learning foreign and second languages: Perspectives in research and scholarship* (pp. 209-237). New York: Modern Language Association.

Byrnes, H. (1991). Reflections on the development of cross-cultural communicative competence in the foreign language classroom. In B. Freed (Ed.), *Foreign language acquisition research and the classroom* (pp. 205-219). Lexington, MA: D. C. Heath.

Davis, R. L. (1997). Group work is NOT busy work: Maximizing success of group work in the L2 classroom. *Foreign Language Annals, 30*, 265-279.

Fantini, A. (1999). Comparisons: Towards the development of intercultural competence. In J. K. Phillips & R. M. Terry (Eds.), *Foreign language standards: Linking research, theories, and practices* (pp. 165-217). Lincolnwood, IL: National Textbook Co.

Felder, R. M., & Henriques, E. R. (1995). Learning and teaching styles in foreign and second language instruction. *Foreign Language Annals, 28*, 21-31.

García, C. (1996). Teaching speech act performance: Declining an invitation. *Hispania, 79*, 267-277.

Hall, J. K. (1999). The communication standards. In J. K. Phillips & R. M. Terry (Eds.), *Foreign language standards: Linking research, theories, and practices* (pp. 15-56). Lincolnwood, IL: National Textbook Co.

Harper, S. N. (1988). Strategies for teaching literature at the undergraduate level. *The Modern Language Journal, 72*, 402-408.

Iandoli, L. J. (1991). Improving oral communication in an interactive introduction to literature course. *Foreign Language Annals, 24*, 479-486.

Klamm, M. (1990). The perfect match: Cooperative learning and foreign languages. *Kansas Foreign Language Association Bulletin*, January, 3-5; April, 3-5; September, 35-36; November, 3-7.

Lange, D. L. (1999). Planning for and using the new national culture standards. In J. K. Phillips & R. M. Terry (Eds.), *Foreign language standards: Linking research, theories, and practices* (pp. 57-120). Lincolnwood, IL: National Textbook Co.

Mantle-Bromley, C. (1992). Preparing students for meaningful culture learning. *Foreign Language Annals, 25*, 117-127.

Moore, Z. (1996). Teaching culture: A study of *piropos*. *Hispania, 79*, 113-120.

Omaggio Hadley, A. (2001). *Teaching language in context* (3rd ed.). Boston: Heinle & Heinle.

Ortuño, M. M. (1991). Cross-cultural awareness in the foreign language class: The Kluckhohn model. *The Modern Language Journal, 75*, 449-459.

Ortuño, M. M. (1994). Teaching language skills and cultural awareness with Spanish paintings. *Hispania, 77*, 500-511.

Oxford, R. L. (1997). Cooperative learning, collaborative learning, and interaction: Three communicative strands in the language classroom. *The Modern Language Journal, 81*, 443-456.

Paulson, D. L. (1996). Evaluation of FL learners' writing ability. *Northeast Conference Newsletter, 34*, 12-15.

Richard-Amato, P. A. (1996). *Making it happen: Interaction in the second language classroom: From theory to practice* (2nd ed.). White Plains, NY: Longman.

Rings, L. (1989). Cultural meaning and structure in conversations and their pedagogical implications. *Foreign Language Annals, 22*, 459-468.

Shklovsky, V. (1965). Art as technique. In L. T. Lemon & M. J. Reis (Eds.), *Russian Formalist Criticism: Four Essays* (pp. 3-24). Lincoln: University of Nebraska Press.

Slavin, R. E. (1990). *Cooperative learning: Theory, research, and practice*. Englewood Cliffs, NJ: Prentice Hall.

Terry, R. M. (1991). Teaching and evaluating writing as a communicative skill. *Northeast Conference Newsletter, 29*, 14-19, 45-47, 54.

Torregrosa, M. (1991). Integrating oral, aural, reading, and writing skills. *Northeast Conference Newsletter, 30*, 18-21, 54.

Vande Berg, C. K. (1990). Americans viewed by the Spanish: Using stereotypes to teach culture. *Hispania, 73*, 518-521.

VanPatten, B. (1996). *Input processing and grammar instruction.* Norwood, NJ: Ablex.

Warschauer, M. (1997). Computer-mediated collaborative learning: Theory and practice. *The Modern Language Journal, 81*, 470-481.

Yanes, J. M. (1992). Comprehensible input via culture-schema: Preparation and inspiration for literary study. *Hispania, 75*, 1348-1354.

Young, D. J. (1991). Activating student background knowledge in a take-charge approach to foreign language reading. *Hispania, 74*, 1124-1132.

Young, D. J. (1993). Processing strategies of foreign language readers: Authentic and edited input. *Foreign Language Annals, 26*, 452-468.

**Appendix**

Strategies for teaching literature:

*Pre-Reading:* schema activation on a related topic (rather than information on the author or work)

*In the Text:* (every decision depends on the evidence on the page, not on what the student or the teacher thinks; what is not in the text may be improvised)

1.  Situation/Circumstances (state in 25 words or less; great opener for composition)
2.  Speaker/tone: What do we know about him/her? Young? Older? What is his/her relationship to the situation? Does (s)he participate in the action? Tone: enthusiastic? frightened? sarcastic? happy? sad? comic? ironic? impassive (neutral)?
3.  Characterization (other characters): What do we know about them, in the text and by means of our own "detective work"? (each group can study one character throughout the work)
4.  Time and Place: Give details. Is it ambiguous, imagined, realistic, symbolic, specific?
5.  Point of View: Through whose "eyes" do we "see" the action or situation? Is it consistent or does it change? Is there more than one at a time? Is it the same as that of the speaker/narrator or not? Does the speaker "see" through the eyes of other characters?
6.  Other techniques/structures that the text uses: repeated elements, parallelism, imagery, etc.

7. Other "voices" that the text/speaker and the characters use (Kramsch's "prior texts"; Bakhtin's *heteroglossia*): religious, medical, military, heroic, academic, psychological, popular, clichés....

8. Indeterminacy: What do we know and not know after reading? What questions do we still have? What is not explicit that we have to infer from the text?

9. Apparent world view (cosmovision): What kind of view of the world does this text give us? Optimistic? Pessimistic? What are the details? Is it metaliterary, i.e., does it talk about its own form or make its artistic form transparent, rather than being "realistic"?

*In the Reader:*

10. Defamiliarization (Shklovsky): We usually take for granted what is all around us; we don't "see" it. What does the text make us "see" with new eyes? Why?

11. Reader response (Iser): What corresponds to our expectations (cultural, textual, and personal) and what works against them? What confirms our expectations or surprises us?

12. Worldview of the reader: How does the way we see the world compare to the representation of the world in the text?

*Outside the Text/ In the Larger World:*

13. Intertextuality: What other books, movies, TV programs, personal experiences are like this? How are they similar and different? Is there actual evidence of other "texts" in this text?

14. Cultural context: How would another person from our culture respond to the people and situations in this text? How might a person from the culture that produced the text respond?

15. Author and circumstances of production: Utilize this at the end, after students have some textual ownership. Is this just one possible reading but not the only nor necessarily the best one?

# 7

# Exploring the Events of World War II and the Holocaust in the French Classroom

**Eileen M. Angelini**
Philadelphia University

> The criminal madness of the Occupiers was backed up by the French people, by the French government. France, home of the Englightment and of the Rights of Man, a nation of welcome and of political asylum. That day France committed the irreparable wrong. Turning away from her promises, she delivered her own protected citizens to their executioner ... 74 trains would leave for Auschwitz; 76,000 individuals would never return. To them we owe an indefeasible debt.
>
> –President Jacques Chirac, July 16, 1995

The role of France during the Holocaust is a subject not commonly included in the curriculum of beginning- and intermediate-level French classes. It has been my experience, however, that not only is this period of history of great interest to university students, but it also adds a dimension of study that is thought-provoking and is likely to have a lasting impact on students' understanding of France and French culture.

Until the early 1990s, there was not a regular foreign language program in place at Philadelphia University (formerly known as Philadelphia College of Textiles and Science). There had been occasional courses offered in German, but these were never fully integrated into the curriculum. In the mid-1980s, however, the university received major funding through a FIPSE (Funding for the Improvement of Post-Secondary Education) Grant to develop a general education program that would be "seamlessly interwoven" with the programs of the professional majors. The resulting general education program, now known as College Studies, requires all students to take courses in either a foreign language or in area studies. Students may choose to take two semesters of a language (or of area studies), or they may elect a combination of one semester of a language and one semester of area studies.

The French courses that I teach are at the beginning and intermediate levels. Students generally have little or no prior language experience, and rarely do they progress beyond the level of Intermediate-High on the ACTFL OPI scale. The fact that I will have most of the students for only two semesters (unless they use their electives to declare a minor in French) makes it imperative for me to create cultural units for them that will be "do-able" and will also have a lasting impact on their educational experience. Although the main focus of the foreign language program at my institution is to prepare students for careers that are primarily business-oriented, I nonetheless find it useful and important to integrate literature and film into my courses. I firmly believe that in order to understand how to interact in any foreign environment, one must have a sense of the country's culture and history. It is in this context that have I created a unit on World War II and the Holocaust.

My reasons for doing so are twofold: To expand upon my doctoral research in the modern French novel, I decided to examine the differences in narrative technique between the pre- and post-World War II periods. I also wanted to teach some of what I had been trained to do in graduate school and not be limited to teaching elementary language courses. Consequently, I began to create a cultural unit that would be based on recent French history and that would at the same time prepare my students to be able to interact more comfortably and intelligently in a business-centered environment in France.

When I first started teaching about World War II and the Holocaust in the spring of 1997, I began with *Visages de la Shoah* (Barnett, 1995) ), the award-winning documentary film by Barbara P. Barnett in which Marcel Jabelot relates his horrifying experiences of survival in Auschwitz and during the Death March. When I suggested to Barnett that my students and I might write to Jabelot to express our reactions to the film, she agreed and offered to be of assistance. The results of our initiative were highly rewarding for everyone involved because Jabelot himself responded:

> Je vous suis très reconnaissant d'avoir montré à vos étudiants la vidéo réalisée par Barbara Barnett. En effet, vous avez ainsi participé à l'oeuvre de sauvegarde de la mémoire de la Shoah et à son enseignement. Pour les victimes du nazisme, ce travail pédagogique est de première importance.
>
> Laissez-moi aussi vous féliciter pour l'excellent français que vos élèves ont utilisé dans leurs lettres. Je vous serais très obligé de vouloir bien leur dire combien j'ai été ému et touché en les lisant. C'est à ce moment que j'ai compris toute l'importance de la vidéo de Barbara.

> *I am very grateful that you have shown Barbara Barnett's video to your students. Indeed, you have participated in saving the memory of the Holocaust and in teaching it. For the victims of the Nazi regime, this pedagogical work is of prime importance.*

> *Let me also congratulate you on the excellent French your stu-*
> *dents used in their letters. I would be very grateful to you if you*
> *would tell your students how much I was moved and touched in*
> *reading their letters. It is now that I understand the importance*
> *of Barbara's video (my translation).*

Until his death in 1999, I maintained regular contact with Jabelot, keeping him abreast of other activities in which I engage my students that relate not only to the Holocaust but also to World War II, the Resistance Movement, and Vichy France.

A major opportunity to develop materials and techniques for introducing the events of World War II and the Holocaust in the French classroom came through my participation in an NEH Summer Seminar at Harvard University: "War and Memory: Postwar Representations of the Occupation and World War II in French Literature, History, and Film." The seminar as described by the director, Susan R. Suleiman, was a perfect fit with the research and teaching project that I had already undertaken:

> [...] this split national identity–the Vichy government of Mar-
> shal Pétain on one side, the Free French Forces of Général de
> Gaulle on the other–makes the problems of cultural memory
> relating to the Occupation period especially acute. For every
> memory that some want to preserve or celebrate, there is an
> equally strong pressure on the part of others to forget or repress.
> In dealing with postwar accounts of this period in France, one is
> always obliged to ask: Whose memory, whose forgetting, and
> why?
>
> For a long time, starting with the end of the war, a number of
> comforting stories had been told about the painful years during
> which France was under German Occupation (1940-1944).
> Among these, one of the most enduring was that a great many
> Frenchmen had participated in the Resistance; another, equally
> powerful story was that the Vichy government had been the "se-
> cret ally" of the Resistance, doing its utmost to obstruct and
> oppose the occupying Germans even while appearing to coop-
> erate with them. Robert Paxton's book, *Vichy France* (1972),
> put an abrupt and definitive end to both of those myths. Re-
> ceived at first with indignation and consternation by French
> historians–many of whom were all the more upset that this painful
> unmasking was the work of an American–*Vichy France* inau-
> gurated a whole new period in French historiography about the
> Occupation years, as well as in French popular perceptions about
> the period. [...] Marcel Ophuls' film, *Le Chagrin et la pitié*

(1970), had similarly been received with outrage by the very people who had commissioned it for French television–in fact, it was not shown on television there until 1981.

Over the past decade, and increasingly since the much discussed trial of Klaus Barbie (1983-1987) that impelled many survivors of that time to publish their testimonies, France has seen a veritable outpouring of monographs, comprehensive histories, biographies, and first-person accounts devoted to those years. Henri Russo, in his excellent study of the evolution of official and popular memories of the Vichy period since 1945 (*Le Syndrome de Vichy*, 1987, 1990), refers to this outpouring as a national "obsession." Obsession or no, we now have a large and varied body of literature in several genres, including films and filmscripts, that can be studied alongside works of history and theoretical reflections.

It was during this seminar that I learned that France is the only country that was defeated by the Germans, was occupied by the Germans, collaborated with the Germans, and then declared victory over the Germans. These extraordinary social upheavals brought about a very difficult post-war recuperation period in France that has lasted to the present day. This period of France's history has also been documented and re-created in a large body of literature and film, materials that I now use in the continuing development of the course on the Holocaust. Students have especially enjoyed reading Marguerite Duras' *La Douleur (The War)* (1985) that portrays Resistance fighters and hidden children; Georges Perec's *W ou le souvenir d'enfance (W or the Memory of Childhood)* (1975) and Joseph Joffo's *Un Sac de billes (A Bag of Marbles)* (1973), both of which depict the war through the eyes of a Jewish boy; and the poetry of Charlotte Delbo, a Catholic Resistance fighter who was deported to Auschwitz. Favorite feature-length films have been Louis Malle's *Au revoir les enfants (Goodbye, Children)* (1987) and Jean-Louis Lorenzi's *Le Chambon: La colline aux mille enfants (Le Chambon: Hill of a Thousand Children)* (1994). My objective in teaching is to focus on different modes of artistic expression in order to provide students with a better awareness of life in pre- and post-World War II France. In the beginning French courses, students watch the films with subtitles and have glossed readings from selected texts. In the intermediate courses, students watch the films without subtitles and read non-glossed texts accompanied by a detailed introduction in English. Intermediate students who have been frustrated by the lack of subtitles often come to the university's Language and Cultural Center to watch the film again with subtitles, demonstrating the students' high interest in the subject and motivation to learn. In course evaluations, students have continually and unanimously written that the cultural unit on the events of WWII and the Holocaust has been their favorite and most rewarding.

The catalyst for introducing the events of WWII and the Holocaust into my French classes has been the *Standards for Foreign Language Learning in the 21ˢᵗ Century* (National Standards in Foreign Language Education Project, 1999). It is particularly important to me to show students that French is not a subject to be taught in isolation. I want them to be able to make connections between their French class and their other courses. My article, "Putting the Standards into Practice: Activities for the Foreign Language Classroom," describes some of the interdisciplinary benefits of teaching the Holocaust in the foreign language classroom (Angelini, 1999).

To encourage other colleagues to follow the lead in exploring the events of WWII and the Holocaust in the French classroom, I have co-authored with Barnett an instructor's resource manual that has been funded by a Title VI grant and can be found in its entirety on the AATF Web site, <http://aatf.utsa.edu/>. The goal of the manual is to provide as much useful information as possible for others who may want to explore the topic. For example, the list of Holocaust resource centers includes centers from across the United States as well as those in Canada and France. The resource manual also lists centers that provide information and nationwide services, such as helping to locate and contact WWII veterans and Holocaust survivors.

What follows this article is a compilation of resources that pertain directly to France: (1) a chronology of major events, (2) a glossary of terms, (3) an annotated list of various kinds of materials, and (4) suggested classroom activities and projects. Interested readers may also consult the AATF Web site to find examples of authentic documents and speeches, a list of useful Web addresses, a listing of WWII memorials in France, and a listing of sources for retail sales, i.e., for films and books. These materials and resources are by no means intended to be exhaustive but should be viewed as a springboard for future research and as an inspiration for incorporating the lessons of tolerance and cross-cultural understanding into our classes.

Because teaching the Holocaust lends itself to an interdisciplinary focus, teachers from a wide variety of subject areas such as foreign languages, history, literature, and social sciences will benefit. It is my hope that this article will serve as a resource to help foster collaborative efforts among those who, in the words of Jabelot, wish to join efforts in "saving the memory of the Holocaust and teaching it."

## References

Angelini, E. (1999). Putting the standards into practice: Activities for the foreign language classroom. In A. G. Nerenz (Ed.), *Standards for a new century* (pp. 117-129). Lincolnwood, IL: National Textbook Company.

Barnett, B. (1995). *Visages de la Shoah* [Videocassette]. Rosemont, PA: The Agnes Irwin School.

Duras, M. (1985). *La douleur.* Paris: P.O.L.

Joffo, J. (1973). *Un Sac de billes.* Paris: Editions Jean-Claude Lattès.

Lorenzi, J.-L. (1994). *Le Chambon: La colline aux mille enfants* [Videocassette]. Worcester, PA: Gateway Films.

Malle, L. (1987). *Au revoir les enfants* [Videocassette]. New York: Orion Home Video.

National Standards in Foreign Language Education Project. (1999). *Standards for foreign language learning in the 21$^{st}$ century.* Lawrence, KS: Allen Press.

Ophuls, R. (1970). *Le chagrin et la pitié* [DVD]. Chatsworth, CA: Milestone Film & Video.

Paxton, R. (1972). *Vichy France: Old guard and new order, 1940-1944.* New York: Alfred A. Knopf.

Perec, G. (1975) *W ou le souvenir d'enfance.* Paris: Editions Denoël.

Russo, H. (1987, 1990 ). *Le syndrome de Vichy de 1944 à nos jours.* Paris: Seuil.

## I. CHRONOLOGY

### 1894-1906

The Dreyfus Affair exposes strong antisemitism present in the French military establishment.

### 1939

September 1:  Germany invades Poland.

September 3:  Great Britain and France declare war on Germany.

### 1940

June 12:  France capitulates to Germany.

June 14:  The Germans enter Paris.

June 18:  General Charles DeGaulle calls from London for continued resistance.

June 22:  France surrenders to Germany; France is demilitarized and Germany occupies three fifths of the country.

July:  The French government moves to Vichy, giving full powers to Maréchal Henri Philippe Pétain.

**1941**

> May:  The first roundups of foreign Jews in France take place.
> June:  Germany invades Russia; the "Statuts des Juifs" (antisemitic laws) are enacted by the Vichy government.

**1942**

> May:  A yellow star becomes obligatory for Jews in the Occupied Zone.
> July 16-17:  Approximately 13,000 Jews (including 4,000 children) are detained in the Vélodrome d'Hiver (indoor bicycle arena) in Paris.
> November 11:  The German army invades Vichy France, the Unoccupied Zone.

**1943**

> January:  A French "milice" (militia) is created to support the German Occupation forces against the French Resistance.
> September 8:  Italy surrenders; the Germans enter Nice and begin to deport Jews.
> October:  DeGaulle is recognized as the head of "Free France."

**1944**

> June 6:  The Allies land in Normandy.
> August 25:  Paris is liberated.

**1945**

> January 18:  The Germans evacuate Auschwitz and begin the Death March.
> January 27:  The Russian army liberates Auschwitz.
> May 8:  Germany surrenders; the war in Europe ends.

**1995**

> July 16:  President Jacques Chirac acknowledges France's role in the Holocaust.

**1997**

> September 30:  The French Catholic Church apologizes for its silence during the Holocaust.

## II. GLOSSARY

See especially: Epstein, E. J. & Rosen, P. (1997) *Dictionary of the Holocaust: Biography, geography, and terminology.* Westport, CT: Greenwood Press.

**Antisemites (Antisémites)**
   The people whose actions and feelings are characterized by dislike or hatred for Jews. Antisemitism during WWII resulted in discrimination, persecution, and identification of Jews to Nazi authorities. The Nazis attempted to exterminate all Jews living in Europe.

**"Arbeit Macht Frei" ("Work Makes Free")**
   A sign at the entrance of several concentration camps including Auschwitz, Dachau, Theresienstadt, and Buchenwald.

**Aryan**
> A member of the "master race" (strong, tall, blue-eyed, blond), according to Adolph Hitler.

**Aryanization (Aryanisation)**
> The Nazi expropriation of Jewish property and businesses.

**Auschwitz-Birkenau**
> The largest of the Nazi extermination camps, which was located in Poland.

**Barbie, Klaus, le "boucher de Lyon" ("the butcher of Lyons")**
> A Gestapo leader stationed in Lyons who was responsible for the murder of French Resistance leader Jean Moulin and many Jewish children. Barbie was convicted in France in 1987 for "crimes against humanity."

**Benoit, Abbé Marie**
> A French priest in Marseilles who smuggled more than 4,000 Jews to safety.

**Bousquet, René**
> The Secretary General of the French National Policy in Vichy who was responsible for ordering the Vélodrome d'hiver roundup (q.v.). He was assassinated in 1993 before being brought to trial for "crimes against humanity."

**Brunner, Alois**
> The SS major, head of Drancy internment camp, and assistant to Eichmann (q.v.). He was responsible for sending more than 23,000 Jews from France to Auschwitz.

**Buna-Monowice**
> A slave labor camp in Poland, also called Auschwitz III.

**Chambon-sur-Lignon, le**
> A small farming village in central France (*Haute-Loire*) whose largely Huguenot population saved thousands of Jews (including American filmmaker, Pierre Sauvage).

**CIMADE (Comité Inter-Mouvement auprès des Evacués)**
> A French organization responsible for rescuing Jews and escorting them to Switzerland.

**Concentration Camp (un camp de concentration)**
> A camp where political enemies, prisoners of war, and interned foreigners were held. The Nazis relocated Jews, gypsies, Resistance fighters, and other groups considered a threat to the Nazis. The camps were severely overcrowded, and prisoners suffered from malnutrition and sickness. Prisoners of the concentration camps were frequently abused and killed. Six concentration camps were also death camps, centers of murder and extermination: Auschwitz, Treblinka, Sobibor, Majdanek, Chelmo, and Belzec.

**CRIF (Comité Représentatif des Israélites de France)**
> A French organization representing major Jewish institutions.

**Death March (la marche de la mort)**
A forced march toward the center of Germany when Russian troops approached. The Nazis destroyed the gas chambers at Auschwitz and tried to evacuate concentration camps to obliterate evidence of their extermination policy. Prisoners on death marches were forced to walk long distances without food, water, or satisfactory clothing. Many died or were shot by guards along the way.

**Denounce (dénoncer)**
To turn in Jews and others considered undesirable to the SS (q.v.) or the Gestapo. People who were denounced were usually taken prisoner by the Nazis and deported to concentration camps.

**Deportation (la déportation)**
The resettlement of Jews and other groups from France to concentration camps and extermination camps in Germany, Poland, and Eastern Europe. French officials and police helped Nazis find Jews and other "undesirables."

**Drancy**
The transit camp just outside Paris (*Seine-St. Denis*) where Jews were held before being deported to Auschwitz. It was used for internment of Jews from 1941-1944. Before the war, Drancy served as a police barracks.

**Dreyfus Affair**
A controversial political and judicial scandal that began in 1894 when Captain Alfred Dreyfus, a Jew from Alsace, was found guilty of treason. Pardoned in 1899, he was eventually restored to his rank, promoted, and decorated. Political opponents of Dreyfus were known for their antisemitism, and the affair aroused a wave of antisemitism in France.

**Eichmann, Adolph**
A Lieutenant Colonel in the SS and a mass murderer. He was tried and hanged in Israel in 1962 for "crimes against humanity."

**Final Solution (la solution finale)**
The extermination of all Jews.

**Free Zone (la zone libre)**
The southern two fifths of France, which was not occupied by the Nazis prior to 1943. Many Jews left Paris for the "Free Zone," where they sought refuge from the Nazis and French police.

**Fry, Varian**
An American rescuer and "righteous Gentile" (q.v.) who saved more than 4,000 people from the Nazis, many of whom were prominent scholars, writers, and artists.

**Gas Chamber (la chambre à gaz)**
A tightly sealed room in which Jews were killed when poisonous gas was pumped into the chamber.

**Genocide (le génocide)**
The systematic killing of an ethnic, religious, or national group.

**Gerlier, Cardinal Pierre-Marie**
The Archbishop of Lyons and "righteous Gentile" (q.v.) who ordered Catholic institutions to hide Jewish children.

**Gestapo (la Gestapo)**
The German secret police force that rounded up Jews living in France for deportation to Auschwitz.

**Glasberg, Alexandre (Abbé)**
A Catholic priest converted from Judaism who helped rescue Jews.

**Goy (un "goy")**
A Yiddish term for a non-Jew.

**Gurs**
A French internment camp located in southwestern France near Oloron-Sainte-Marie (*Pyrénées Atlantiques*), used to house non-French Jews prior to deportation.

**Hautval, Dr. Adélaïde**
A French doctor and "righteous Gentile" deported to Auschwitz.

**Hitler, Adolph**
The leader of the Nazi party from 1919-1945; the Führer and leader of the German racist state.

**Holocaust (l'holocauste)**
The destruction of European Jews.

**Internment Camp (un camp d'internement)**
A camp in which foreigners, prisoners of war, or others considered dangerous to pursuing the war effort were confined during wartime.

**Jew (un Juif)**
A pejorative term marked on the yellow star worn by Jews in Occupied France beginning in June, 1942.

**Kapo (un kapo)**
A leader of the block or barracks in concentration camps. Recruited by the Nazis, the Kapos were often Jews chosen so as to create dissent among the camp internees.

**Klarsfeld, Serge and Beate**
Post-war Nazi hunters in Paris. They dedicated their lives to hunting down Nazi war criminals and to documenting the deportations of Jews from France. They were instrumental in the eventual arrest of Klaus Barbie.

**Laval, Pierre**
The Vice-Premier of the Vichy regime who was appointed in 1942. He was tried by a French court and hanged in 1945. He was responsible for deporting men, women, and children.

**Leguay, Jean**
The Vichy police chief who was director of transit camps in the French Occupied Zone.

**Les Milles**

A detention camp in southern France, near Aix-en-Provence (*Bouches-du-Rhône*), that was used to house over 2,000 Germans (mostly artists, intellectuals, and sports figures) who had fled the Nazi regime. After the defeat of France in 1940, the Vichy government planned to send the refugees back to Germany, but the camp's commander refused. A 1995 film, *Les Milles*, depicts their carefully planned escape.

**Liberation (la Libération)**

The liberation of Paris by Allied forces. General Charles DeGaulle marched victoriously into Paris on August 25, 1944.

**Majdanek**

A death camp located near Lublin, Poland.

**Maquis (le Maquis)**

The French underground that was active in the Massif Central.

**Mauthausen**

A concentration camp in Linz, Austria.

**Milice (la milice)**

The pro-Nazi French paramilitary of 30,000 formed in 1943 to support Pétain and the German Occupation.

**Monowice**

A Polish town and slave labor factory near Auschwitz.

**Moulin, Jean**

The leader of the French Resistance. He was arrested and tortured by the Gestapo in Lyons in 1943 and later died during his deportation to Germany. His ashes were transferred to the Panthéon in 1964.

**Odessa**

A Russian port in Ukraine on the Black Sea.

**OSE (Oeuvre de Secours aux Enfants israélites)**

An organization for the rescue of Jewish children.

**Papon, Maurice**

A Vichy official involved in deporting 1,690 Jews. He was convicted in 1998 for "crimes against humanity."

**Pétain, Maréchal Henri Philippe**

The French leader of the Vichy regime. After the fall of France in 1940, the National Assembly voted to suspend the constitutional laws of the Third Republic and gave World War I hero Maréchal Pétain full power as Head of State. The new government of Unoccupied France made its capital in the resort town of Vichy in south central France.

**Pithiviers**

A French internment and transit camp 65 miles south of Paris near Orléans (*Loiret*).

**Resistance (la Résistance)**

The organized opposition to Nazi Occupation.

**Righteous Gentiles (les "justes")**
Christians who risked their lives to save Jews and who were later honored by Yad Vashem (q.v.) in Israel.

**Rivesaltes**
A French internment camp in southern France near Perpignan (*Pyrénées Orientales*).

**Saliège, Monsignor Jules-Gérard**
The Archbishop of Toulouse who actively opposed the Vichy government's anti-Jewish measures.

**Shoah (la Shoah)**
The Hebrew word for the Holocaust.

**SS (acronym for *Schutzstaffel*)**
The Nazi paramilitary police organization created in 1925 to assure Hitler's personal protection.

**Statuts des Juifs**
The Antisemitic laws issued by the Vichy government in October, 1940. These laws defined who was Jewish in the eyes of the French state and excluded Jews from top positions in government, education, broadcasting, journalism, theater, and the military.

**Vélodrome d'hiver ("le Vel d'hiv")**
An indoor bicycle arena in Paris, where more than 13,000 Jews were kept after being rounded up on July 16 and 17, 1942. After being held three days at the Vel d'hiv, the Jews were transported to Auschwitz. The roundup of the Vel d'hiv has become a symbol of French collaboration in the deportation and eventual extermination of Jews living in France. On July 16, France annually commemorates the deportation of the Jews at an official ceremony in the Place des Martyrs Juifs in Paris.

**Vichy France (la France de Vichy)**
The government of France under the leadership of Maréchal Pétain. After France surrendered in 1940 and Germans had occupied of three fifths of the country, the French government moved to the city of Vichy. Although the town of Vichy was in the unoccupied part of France, the French government collaborated with Nazi antisemitism and supported the deportations of Jews and other "undesirables."

**Yad Vashem**
The Israeli Holocaust Remembrance Center that honors Holocaust martyrs and heroes. For example, in 1985 Yad Vashem posthumously honored Father Jacques (cf. Louis Malle's *Au revoir les enfants*) as one of the "Righteous Among the Nations."

**Yellow Star (l'Étoile Jaune)**
The symbol worn by Jews in France and other European countries. Jews were required by law to wear the yellow six-pointed star embroidered with the word *Juif*.

## III. PRINT AND MEDIA RESOURCES

### A. FILM AND VISUAL CULTURE

#### 1. Documentaries

Barnett, B. (Director). (1995). *Visages de la Shoah (Faces of the Holocaust)* [Videocassette]. 59 minutes. Rosemont, PA: The Agnes Irwin School.
French Holocaust survivor, Marcel Jabelot, relates his experiences of survival in Auschwitz and during the Death March. The film is done in an interview format accompanied by authentic World War II archival photographs. The film won an Honorable Mention Award at the University of California-Berkeley Film Festival in 1995.

Chabrol, C. (Director). (1996). *L'oeil de Vichy (The eye of Vichy)* [Videocassette]. 110 minutes. New York: First Run Features Home Video.
Examples of Vichy-produced propaganda items, newsreels, and movie excerpts brilliantly illustrate the nature of Vichy ideology and collaboration.

Doillon, J. (Director). (1975). *Un sac de billes (A bag of marbles)* [Videocassette]. Paris: Renn Productions, Les Films Christian Fechner.
Although based on Joseph Joffo's autobiography of the same title (q.v.), the film fails to capture the charm of the written text. However, it does show scenes of the Occupation that might not otherwise be known, especially those of hidden children and the hardships they endured.

Gardner, R. (Director). (1986). *The courage to care* [Videocassette]. 28 minutes. Alexandria, VA: United Way.
This film shows how ordinary people refused to succumb to the Nazis and rescued Holocaust victims. It includes interviews with the late Magda Trocmé and Nelly Trocmé Hewett, wife and daughter of Pastor André Trocmé of Le Chambon-sur-Lignon. The film was nominated for an Academy Award in 1986 for best short documentary film.

Gossels, L. (Producer). (1999). *Children of Chabannes* [Videocassette]. 92 minutes. New York: Perennial Pictures, Inc.
People in the tiny village of Chabannes chose action over indifference and saved the lives of 400 Jewish refugee children. See also: <http://www.childrenofchabannes.org/>.

Hartz, R. K. (Director). (1997). *A legacy of goodness: French rescuers during World War II* [Videocassette]. 28 minutes. Elkins Park, PA: *Your Name is Renée* Institute.
Ruth Kapp Hartz was a hidden child in France. Her saviors (and their descendants) had a strong desire to promote the importance of remembering those who courageously helped French Jews survive. This video is an excellent follow-up to Cretzmeyer's biography of Hartz (q.v.) and is available from *Your Name is Renée* Institute, 512 St. James Place, Elkins Park, PA.

Kaplan, R. (Director). (1997). *Assignment rescue* [Videocassette]. 26 minutes. New York: Richard Kaplan Productions. Available : <http://www.buyindies.com/listings/2/8/FCTS-28173.html>.

The American journalist, Varian Fry, assisted in rescuing 200 famous intellectual refugees from the hands of the Nazis at the start of World War II and helped them leave Europe via Marseilles, France. Those rescued by Fry include writers André Breton and Hannah Arendt, as well as artists Marc Chagall, Marcel Duchamp, and Max Ernst. Also available is Fry's autobiography, *Assignment Rescue* (q.v.).

Lanzmann, C. (Director). (1986). *Shoah* [5 Videocassettes]. 9 hours 30 minutes. Hollywood, CA: Paramount Home Video.

Lanzmann's goal in *Shoah* is to depict the inhumanity of the Final Solution (1942-1944) through oral testimony. One of the most striking aspects of the film is the footage taken by Lanzmann in Poland. Because of the length of the film, the complete text with its preface by Simone de Beauvoir is extremely helpful.

Ophuls, M. (Director). (1970). *Le chagrin et la pitié (The sorrow and the pity)* [DVD]. 260 minutes. Chatsworth, CA: Milestone Film & Video.

To quote Susan R. Suleiman, this is the "groundbreaking documentary on the Occupation years in France." *Le Chagrin et la pitié* led the way for the reexamination of France's role in World War II at both the national and local levels.

Ophuls, M. (Director). (1989). *Hotel Terminus: The life and times of Klaus Barbie* [Videocassette]. 267 minutes. Santa Monica, CA: MGM Home Entertainment.

The former Gestapo agent, Klaus Barbie, was only recently condemned for crimes against humanity. Particularly haunting in this film are scenes from his "hidden life" after World War II and from his trial in France.

Resnais, A. (Director). (1955). *Nuit et brouillard (Night and fog)* [Videocassette]. 32 minutes. Chicago: Home Vision Video.

With haunting music and voice-overs, this documentary proves the existence of the German concentration camps during World War II. Footage includes scenes showing the medical experiments to which the Jews were subjected as well scenes of the liberation of the camps.

Sauvage, P. (Director). (1988). *Weapons of the spirit* [Videocassette]. 120 minutes. New York: First Run Features Home Video.

Pierre Sauvage retraces his roots to a small Protestant town, Le Chambon, in south central France. The people and the clergy of Le Chambon united to protect thousands of Jews from the Nazis and the collaborators in the Vichy government. A good companion guide to *Weapons of the Spirit* is Philip Hallie's book, *Lest Innocent Blood Be Shed* (q.v.).

## 2. Fiction and Feature Films

Audiard, J. (Director). (1998*). Un héros très discret (A discreet hero)* [Videocassette]. 105 minutes. New York: New Yorker Video.
    After World War II, a young Frenchman invents a heroic past with the French Resistance. As a result, he becomes a reputable officer in the French Army.

Berri, C. (Director). (1991). *Uranus* [Videocassette]. 100 minutes. New York: HBO Video (Prestige).
    Based on Marcel Aymé's novel, *Uranus* depicts a small rural town in post-Liberation France that still has not recuperated from the destruction brought about by wartime bombing and where the Communists have assumed power. For these Communists, sniffing out Nazi collaborators is foremost on the agenda. Tensions mount as it becomes increasingly difficult to ascertain who had been a Nazi collaborator, a Resistance fighter, or someone with no particular political allegiance who simply tried to survive the war.

Berri, C. (Director). (1997). *Lucie Aubrac* [Videocassette]. 111 minutes. Paris: Pathé Vidéo.
    Based on Lucie Aubrac's book, *Ils partiront dans l'ivresse (Outwitting the Gestapo)*, this film, with poetic license, focuses on Aubrac's efforts to free her husband from the Gestapo, an effort in which she is assisted by other members of the Resistance. The film also portrays the passionate and loving relationship between Aubrac and her husband.

Chabrol, C. (Director). (1998). *Une affaire de femmes (Women's business)* [Videocassette]. 110 minutes. New York: New Yorker Video.
    During the Occupation, a man returns from captivity to find that his wife has acquired a profitable side job of performing abortions. The film is based on the true story of Marie Latour, the last woman to be executed under the death penalty in France.

Clements, R. (Director). (1952). *Les jeux interdits (Forbidden games)* [Videocassette]. 105 minutes. Chicago: Home Vision Cinema.
    As a young French family desperately tries to escape to the Free Zone of France during World War II, a German air raid tragically orphans the little girl. She is taken in by a peasant family and becomes fast friends with the family's young son. Their games naively imitate the tragedies of the war around them.

De Chalonge, C. (Director). (1990). *Docteur Petiot* [Videocassette]. 102 minutes. Los Angeles: World Artists Home Video.
    The film is based on the true story of the French physician who lured desperate Jews trying to escape Nazi-occupied France, only to steal everything they owned and then murder them in his own private crematorium.

Drach, M. (Director). (1974). *Les violons du bal (The violins of the ball)* [Videocassette]. 105 minutes. Santa Monica, CA: Connoisseur Video Collection.
    A fictional filmmaker remembers his youth as a Jewish child during the Occupation of France.

Favart, M. (Director). (1996). *Les Alsaciens ou les deux Mathilde* [Videocassette]. 6 hours 40 minutes. Paris: Pathé Vidéo.

Focusing on the struggles of the people of the Alsace region as they are shuffled back and forth between being part of France and of Germany, this telefilm traces the history of four generations of a family from the time of the war with Prussia in the 19th century to World War II. The strength of the production lies in its portrayal of conflicts with national and linguistic identity in Strasbourg, a hotbed of action between the Resistance fighters and the Nazi collaborators. The 1996 novel by DeTurenne & Ducher was based on this telefilm.

Finkiel, E. (Director). (2000). *Voyages* [Videocassette]. 115 minutes. Paris: La Sept Vidéo.

This film sensitively depicts the contemporary experiences of three female Holocaust survivors. Riwka, age 65, a French woman who has long been living in Israel, takes a tour of Poland where the bus breaks down in the middle of nowhere. Régine, age 65, who lives alone in Paris, receives a letter from a man in Lithuania claiming to be her father, whom she always assumed had died in the camps. Vera, age 85, a tireless émigré from Russia, traverses Israel in search of her lost cousin and is bemused by the fact that no one in the Jewish homeland speaks a word of Yiddish.

Grall, S. (Director). (1995). *Les Milles* [Film]. 103 minutes. Paris: CiBy Distributors.

A French military officer single-handedly requisitions a train to transport hundreds of German refugees to neutral territory rather than hand them over to certain death under the terms of the newly-signed Franco-German armistice of June, 1940.

Granier-Deferre, P. (Director). (1973). *Le train* [Videocassette]. 120 minutes. [s.l.]: VIP International.

This sentimental drama with Jean-Louis Trintignant, Romy Schneider, and Maurice Biraud focuses on the German Occupation of France and a man who, separated from his wife, is drawn to a stranger on a crowded train.

Kurys, D. (Director). (1983). *Entre nous (Between us)* [Videocassette]. 112 minutes. New York: Fox/Lorber Home Video.

Two women meet after the end of World War II and subsequently fall in love with one another. The first woman had been in a Jewish detention camp in the south of France when she met her husband. The second woman's fiancé had been killed in a German raid of her university. Their relationship builds upon their suffering because of World War II. This film is unique in its showing of the French detention camps and the lesser-known victims of the war.

Lelouche, C. (Director). (1995). *Les misérables du XXe siècle ('Les misérables' of the 20th century)* [Videocassette]. 175 minutes. London: Warner Home Video.

A courageous man faces trials and tribulations when he tries to help a Jewish family during the Occupation.

Lorenzi, J.-L. (Director). (1994). *Le Chambon: La colline aux mille enfants (Le Chambon: Hill of a thousand children)* [Videocassette]. 118 minutes. Worcester, PA: Gateway Films.

The citizens of the village of Le Chambon-sur-Lignon are farmers of Huguenot descent. Understanding the trauma of religious persecution, they vow to help as many Jews as possible escape from the Nazis. Led by Pastor André Trocmé, they miraculously win the battle with their "weapons of the spirit."

Losey, J. (Director). (1976). *Monsieur Klein* [Videocassette]. 124 minutes. Paris: Carrera Vidéo.

In a case of carefully planned mistaken identity, a Frenchman who is Roman Catholic by birth profits enormously from the Occupation. When he is questioned by the Gestapo, he must desperately try to prove he is not Jewish or he will be deported.

Malle, L. (Director). (1974). *Lacombe Lucien* [Videocassette]. 132 minutes. Radlett, England: Arrow Films.

A misdirected country youth, who wants to be with those who have guns, finds himself with a group of Nazi collaborators. The story has a dramatic turn of events when the young man falls in love with the daughter of a Jewish tailor. The film script is also available.

Malle, L. (Director). (1987). *Au revoir les enfants (Goodbye, children)* [Videocassette]. 104 minutes. New York: Orion Home Video.

A student in a Catholic boarding school (a young Louis Malle) befriends a Jewish boy who is being hidden from the Germans. Tragedy strikes when the true identity of the boy is discovered.

Melville, J.-P. (Director). (1997). *Le silence de la mer (The silence of the sea)* [Videocassette]. 86 minutes. [s.l.]: MKS Videos.

Adapted from Vercors' novella, *Le Silence de la mer* is a sensitive rendering of the hardship faced by an uncle and his niece when they are forced to billet a Nazi officer. Although uncle and niece vow never to speak to him, the Nazi officer tells them his innermost thoughts and feelings about France and the war. When he believes he has finally reached an understanding with them, the officer is ordered to the Eastern front.

Miller, C. (Director). (1992). *L'accompagnatrice (The accompanist)* [Videocassette]. 111 minutes. Burbank, CA: Columbia TriStar Home Video.

A Parisian merchant sees collaboration with the Nazis as a means to increase his wealth. However, he is married to a beautiful and famous singer who has an illicit affair with the leader of the French Resistance. The interactions among these colorful characters are seen through the eyes of the innocent young pianist who sacrifices her own chance at musical success by continuing to work for the wife.

Resnais, A. (Director). (1959). *Hiroshima mon amour* [Videocassette]. 86 minutes. Chicago: Home Vision Cinema.
Living in Japan and linked by an amorous relationship, a Japanese architect
and a French actress share memories of World War II from their very different perspectives. Her past includes a love affair with a German soldier during
the Occupation and the shame it brought upon her family. The film includes
footage of the aftermath of the bombing of Hiroshima and shows the museums that Japan has built as a memorial. The story is also available in written
form: Duras, M. (1998). *Hiroshima mon amour*. Paris: Éditions Gallimard.
Truffaut, F. (Director). (1980). *Le dernier métro (The last train)* [Videocassette].
131 minutes. New York: Fox/Lorber Home Video
In Paris during the Occupation, an actress continues to direct the theater company previously directed by her Jewish husband. It is believed that he has
escaped from France, but in reality he is hidden in the basement of the theater.
The film script is also available.

## 3. Film Scripts (complete written scenarios)

Lanzmann, C. (1985). *Shoah*. New York: Pantheon Books.
Malle, L. & Modiano, P. (1974). *Lacombe Lucien*. Paris: Gallimard.
Malle, L. (1988). *Au revoir les enfants*. Paris: L'Avant-Scène.
Truffaut, François. (1983). *Le dernier métro*. Paris: L'Avant-Scène.

## 4. Critical Commentaries

Armes, R. (1989). Cinema of paradox: French film-making during the Occupation. In G. Hirschfeld & P. Marsh (Eds.), *Collaboration in France: Politics in
culture during the Nazi Occupation, 1940-44* (pp. 126-141). Oxford/New York/
Munich: Berg International.
Armes provides an overview of the production of the approximately 200 French
films that appeared during the Occupation and reviews postwar assessments
of their quality, stressing the difficulty of evaluating the ideological content
of individual films produced under multiple wartime constraints.
Avisar, I. (1988). *Screening the Holocaust: Cinema's images of the unimagin-
able*. Bloomington: Indiana University Press.
Not limited to French cinema, this work also includes an excellent analysis of
*Night and Fog*.
Barnes, R. (1992). Vercors: Morality and commitment. *Modern and Contemporary France, 50*, 3-10.
Barnes assesses the legacy of Jean Bruller (Vercors), author of the Occupa-
tion classic, *Le Silence de la mer,* on the occasion of the dedication of the
Vercors memorial plaque on the Pont des Arts (Paris) in February, 1992. Barnes
focuses on Vercors' postwar sympathy for and his later criticisms of the Com-
munist Party, and he sees the criticism as more in keeping with the spirit of
Vercors' fiction.

Braunschweig, M. & Gidel, B. (1989). *Les déportés d'Avon: Enquête autour du film de Louis Malle 'Au revoir les enfants.'* Paris: La Découverte.
Braunschweig, a teacher of history in Avon (Fontainebleau), has her classes study Louis Malle's film, *Au Revoir les enfants*. More than 40 years after the end of the war, they live in the same town as the Catholic boarding school attended by Malle and the three Jewish boys arrested by the Gestapo. Particularly interesting is the differentiation the author makes between reality and artistic liberty taken by the filmmaker.
Brosman, C. S. (1999). *Visions of war in France: Fiction, art, ideology*. Baton Rouge: Louisiana State University Press.
This work critically examines literary representations of war in France by a variety of authors and artists. It explores pertinent literary representations through disparate intellectual, ideological, and historical contexts.
Colombat, A. (1993). *The Holocaust in French film*. Metuchen, NJ: The Scarecrow Press.
Extremely well documented and informative, this is one of the few books devoted to the Holocaust in French film. The directors discussed include Resnais, Ophuls, Malle, Losey, Lanzmann, and Sauvage.
Insdorf, A. (1989). *Indelible shadows: Film and the Holocaust*. Cambridge: Cambridge University Press.
This work is not limited to French cinema and includes analyses of *Le Dernier Métro*, *Les Violons du bal*, *Lacombe Lucien*, and *Night and Fog*.

*B. MUSIC*

The following three CDs are available at <http://www.amazon.com>. The search must include the name of the publisher (i.e., "Arkadia" for the first CD and "Forlane" for the second and third).

Arkadia (Publisher). *Les chansons sous l'Occupation: French songs of World War II* [CD].
This recording includes music by guitarist, Django Reinhardt.
Forlane (Publisher). *Quand la vie sépare ceux qui s'aiment (1939–1940). La vie quotidienne en chansons sous la drôle de guerre et l'Occupation, 2* [CD].
Forlane (Publisher). *De la propagande vichyssoise à l'optimisme de rigueur (1940–1942). La vie quotidienne en chansons sous la drôle de guerre et l'Occupation, 3* [CD].
Although some may consider both Forlane CDs "saccharine," the historical richness is not to be overlooked. Volume 2 includes songs by Tino Rossi and Maurice Chevalier, both tainted as collaborators (Chevalier performed in Germany for POWs in exchange for protection of his Jewish mistress and her parents who were hiding in the south of France). Volume 3 contains the popular hit, "Maréchal nous voilà," which is riddled with fascist themes.

## C. LITERATURE

### 1. Novels and Short Stories (Fiction)

Céline, L.-F. (1957). *D'un château à l'autre*. Paris: Éditions Gallimard.
Céline, controversial for his fascist political affiliations but published in the Pléiade editions because of his literary talent, gives an autofictional account of those Nazi collaborators in the French government who were hidden in a castle in the south of Germany from the time of the Allied invasion of France in 1944 to the fall of Berlin in 1945.

DeTurenne, H. & Ducher, F. (1996). *Les Alsaciens ou les deux Mathilde*. Paris: Éditions Jean-Claude Lattès.
This novel was based on Favart's earlier telefilm of the same title (q.v.).

Duras, M. (1985*). La douleur*. Paris: P.O.L.
Duras' collection of six short stories ("La douleur," "Monsieur X. dit ici Pierre Rabier," "Albert des Capitales," "Ter le milicien," "L'Ortie brisée," and "Aurélia Paris") presents the horrors of the Occupation through a variety of different perspectives (e.g., through the eyes of Resistance fighters and those of a hidden child). The first two stories can be seen as "autofictional" narratives by Duras. For example, in the first story, "La douleur," she recounts the agonizing time spent waiting for the return of her husband, Robert Anthelme, who was deported. The story also tells how François Mitterrand found Anthelme.

Modiano, P. (1968). *La place de l'étoile*. Paris: Éditions Gallimard.
What is fascinating about Modiano's work is that he was born after the end of World War II but writes from the perspective of someone living through the Occupation.

Modiano, P. (1969). *Ronde de nuit*. Paris: Éditions Gallimard.
Particularly intriguing in Modiano's works is this novel where the main character is playing the role of a double spy and must decide whether to help the Resistance fighters or the Nazi collaborators.

Modiano, P. (1997). *Dora Bruder*. Paris: Éditions Gallimard.
From a few clues and photographs, Modiano tries to reconstitute the story of Dora Bruder, a 15-year old who left Drancy on September 18, 1942, on a convoy to Auschwitz. Modiano believes that if he does not tell the story, no trace will remain of her life. This short narrative is an excellent reflection on memory. Written in simple, clear language, the story is moving and powerful.

Perec, G. (1975). *W ou le souvenir d'enfance*. Paris: Éditions Denoël.
This fascinating narrative alternates between Perec's autobiographical accounts of survival as a Jewish child during the Occupation, one who had lost both his father and mother, and the fictional story of the island of W. The island purports to uphold the ideals of the Olympic Games but is simultaneously an allegory for a concentration camp.

Sartre, J.-P. (1981). *La mort dans l'âme*. Paris: Gallimard.
Sartre's third novel of the *Roads to Freedom* series brilliantly portrays the traumas of the French defeat in 1940, the ambiguities of collaboration, and the varied paths to resistance. While the dialogue is often a bit awkward, most of the characters are quite realistically drawn.

Semprun, J. (1963). *Le grand voyage*. Paris: Gallimard.
Semprun, a Spanish exile writing in French, was a Resistant and a Buchenwald survivor. Here he gives a powerful fictionalized account of a journey to the concentration camps.

Simon, C. (1960). *La route des Flandres*. Paris: Éditions du Seuil.
Told in both first- and third-person narration, *La Route des Flandres* depicts the rout of the French in the spring of 1940 when the French cavalry fought German tanks. There are flashbacks to 18th century ancestors, and consequently pride of family heritage comes to the forefront of what the narrator calls the "phony war."

Vercors. (1991). *Le silence de la mer / The silence of the sea* (J. W. Brown & L. D. Stokes, Eds.). Oxford and Washington, DC: Berg International.
This is an excellent annotated bilingual edition of the Vercors novel about the French Resistance. Particularly helpful are the historical and literary introductions, the extensive vocabulary lists, and the select bibliography. (See film of the same title).

## 2. Memoirs, Testimonies, and Biographies

Anthelme, R. (1957). *L'espèce humaine*. Paris: Gallimard.
This narrative by Marguerite Duras' husband, who survived the camps, has become a classic of Holocaust literature.

Aubrac, L. (1993). *Outwitting the Gestapo* (K. Bieber, Trans.). Lincoln: University of Nebraska Press.
Lucie Aubrac gives a horrifying account of her participation in the Resistance in the Vichy Zone. The added benefit to the English translation of the original text (*Ils partiront dans l'ivresse*, Paris: Éditions du Seuil, 1984) is the introduction by Margaret Collins Weitz, author of *Sisters in the Resistance* (q.v.), who presents Aubrac's participation in the Resistance in the broader framework of political and feminist history.

Aubrac, L. (2000). *La Résistance expliquée à mes petits-enfants*. Paris: Editions du Seuil.
Lucie Aubrac answers questions from her grandchildren about the Resistance in France and her experiences in the movement. Written in clear, concise French, this 55-page book is accessible to intermediate or advanced students of French. It is a good accompaniment to the film, *Lucie Aubrac*.

Bellos, D. (1993). *Georges Perec: A life in words*. Boston: David R. Godine.
Bellos provides a detailed yet thoroughly entertaining biography of Georges Perec, recently recognized as one of the greatest French writers of the post-World War II era. The beauty of this biography lies in its portrayal of Perec's childhood during the Occupation. Perec's father died on the front, his mother was deported, and he was sent to the south of France via a Red Cross envoy and hidden in a Catholic boys' school. Bellos also provides insight into Perec's literary genius.

Cayrol, J. (1997). *Alerte aux ombres*. Paris: Seuil.
This is a collection of poems written in secrecy in the concentration camps by the scriptwriter of *Night and Fog*.

Cretzmeyer, S. (1994). *Your name is Renée: Ruth's story as a hidden child*. London: Oxford University Press.
This is a first-person account of a young Jewish child who witnesses the chilling events in France during the Occupation and tells of her saviors who risk their own lives to protect her.

Delbo, C. (1965). *Convoi à Auschwitz*. Paris: Éditions de Minuit.
All of Delbo's narratives deal with her horrifying experience of being deported to Auschwitz and her repatriation into France. Here she gives compelling portraits of her fellow deportees.

Delbo, C. (1971). *Auschwitz et après*. Paris: Éditions de Minuit.
Delbo's poetic style is particularly striking in this trilogy, also available as three separate volumes published by Editions de Minuit: *Aucun de nous ne reviendra* (1970), *Une Connaissance inutile* (1970), and *Mesure de nos jours* (1971).

Delbo, C. *Spectres, mes compagnons (Phantoms, my companions*, R. Lamont, Trans.). (1971). *Massachusetts Review, 12* (1), 23-30.
Delbo tells the story of her journey to Auschwitz accompanied in her imagination by French literary figures: Julien Sorel, Fabrice del Dongo, Ondine, Phèdre, and Molière's Alceste. Their appearance fortifies her. As the train nears its destination (Auschwitz), one by one the figures disappear. Even Molière's misanthrope, Alceste, cannot bear to face the atrocities of the camps, and he also leaves, revealing the impossibility of culture and art amid such misery.

Delbo, C. (1982). Who will carry the word? (C. Haft, Trans.). In R. Skloot (Ed.), *The Theatre of the Holocaust* (pp. 267-325). Madison: University of Wisconsin Press.
Delbo's play portrays the lives of women prisoners in Auschwitz. One of the characters, Claire, encourages her fellow inmates to maintain hope and try to live so that someone will survive to tell the story.

Delbo, C. (1985). *Le mémoire et les jours*. Paris: Berg International.
This work is also published as: *Days and Memory* (R. Lamont, Trans.). (1990). Marlboro, VT: Marlboro Press.

Forché, C. (Ed.). (1993). *Against forgetting: Twentieth-century poetry of witness*. New York: W. W. Norton & Co.

This landmark anthology contains works that examine dark times from more than 140 poets from five continents. It includes many works by French poets on the topic of the Holocaust.

Fry, V. (1967) *Assignment: Rescue: An autobiography*. New York: Scholastic Press.

This autobiography tells the story of Varian Fry, an American secret agent who traveled to France in June of 1940 under the guise of assisting the International YMCA. His real intention was to help smuggle Jews through the tightly controlled French borders. The Jews trapped in southern France would face certain deportation to concentration camps if they did not escape the Gestapo. Fry describes the 13 months he spent helping the enemies of the Third Reich to obtain money, false passports, transportation, and other items necessary for safe travel across France. He is credited with saving the lives of 2,000 to 3,000 people.

Garnier, D. (1980). *Nice, pour mémoire*. Paris: Editions du Seuil.

Hallie, P. (1979). *Lest innocent blood be shed: The story of the village of Le Chambon and how goodness happened there*. New York: Harper & Row, 1979.

The author recounts the story of the heroic people of Le Chambon, a small Protestant town in the south of France. In the face of the Vichy government and a division of the Nazi SS, these people protected thousands of Jews. This book is a wonderful companion to Pierre Sauvage's documentary film, *Weapons of the Spirit* (q.v.).

Joffo, J. (1973). *Un sac de billes*. Paris: Editions Jean-Claude Lattès.

This is the true story of Joseph Joffo who, at the age of 10, escaped from the Occupied Zone to the Free Zone with his 12-year-old brother, Maurice. This autobiography describes the Nazi Occupation as seen through the eyes of a child, a naively innocent perspective (e.g., crossing the line of demarcation between the two zones, little Joseph was upset not to find an "actual" physical line). Joffo also provides critical commentary on the film of the same name directed by Jacques Doillon (q.v.).

Kofman, S. (1994). *Rue Ordener, Rue Labat*. Paris: Éditions Galilée.

Kofman gives her account of survival as a Jewish child during the Occupation and her struggle with the transfer of affection from her mother to the fascinating Catholic woman who hid her and her mother.

Liebster, S. A. (2000). *Facing the lion: Memoirs of a young girl in Nazi Europe*. New Orleans: Grammaton Press.

Before World War II, Simone Arnold was a young girl who delighted in life. In 1942, the Nazis (the "lion") took over Alsace-Lorraine, and Simone's schools became Nazi propaganda machines. Because of her religious beliefs, Simone refused to put the Nazi party above God, and her refusal to say, "Heil

Hitler," led to her persecution by school staff and local officials and rejection by friends. With her father already in a German concentration camp, Simone is wrested from her mother and sent to a reform school to be "reeducated." There she learns that her mother has also been put into a camp.

Mitterrand, F. & Wiesel, E. (1995). *Mémoire à deux voix.* Paris: Éditions Odile Jacob.

France's former President and the Nobel Peace Prize laureate Wiesel share their ideas on a variety of subjects, including their youth, memories of the war years, religion, and literature.

Tichauer, E. (1988). *J'étais le numéro 20832 à Auschwitz.* Paris: Éditions L'Harmattan.

Eva Tichauer was born in Berlin at the end of World War I. When Hitler came to power in 1933, she and her family (German-Jewish socialists and intellectuals) emigrated to Paris. Tichauer was in her second year of medical school when Germany invaded France. She and her mother were deported to Auschwitz via Drancy on July 16, 1942, during the Vel d'hiv roundup. Her father had been arrested in December, 1941. Only Eva survived, and her moving memoir speaks of her misfortune and recovery.

Wiesel, E. (1998). *La nuit.* Paris: Éditions de Minuit.

The Nobel Peace Prize laureate tells of his deportation to Auschwitz, the death of his mother and baby sister in the gas chambers, and the loss of his father in the final days of the Death March.

## 3. Critical Works/Commentaries

Gorrara, C. (1997). Writing and memory: The Occupation and the construction of the self in the 1980's French literature. *Modern and Contemporary France, 5,* 35-45.

Gorrara applies James E. Young's model of memory as an "evolving dialogic relationship with the present" to Lucie Aubrac's *Ils partiront dans l'ivresse* (1984) and Dominique Garnier's *Nice, pour mémoire* (1980). Gorrara finds contrasting but equally valid efforts to reconstruct the past in the two memoirs.

Gorrara, C. (1998). *Women's representations of the Occupation in post-1968 France.* New York: Macmillan.

The author presents a well written, concise study of works that directly address the war years, all written by French women. Beginning with an overview of historical and literary narratives of the war years from 1945 to the present, Gorrara then discusses women resisters' autobiographies; the more radical works by Frédérique Moret, Violette Maurice, and Marguerite Duras; the works of Clara Malraux; and writing by "daughters of the Occupation," including daughters of resisters, collaborators, and deported Jews.

Haft, C. (1973). *The theme of Nazi concentration camps in French literature.* The Hague: Mouton.

Although perhaps dated in its use of myth to interpret literature, this book draws heavily upon works of Charlotte Delbo, whom Haft was able to interview extensively.

Higgins, L. & Holquist, M. *New novel, new wave, new politics: Fiction and the representation of history in post-war France.* Lincoln: University of Nebraska Press.

This work overturns the traditional approach of previous studies of the film and literature that emerged in France in the mid-1950s, studies that concentrated on formal innovations. The authors argue that the new novelists and filmmakers "engage in a kind of historiography" and "enact the conflicts, the double binds of postwar history and representation." They give a dramatic revisioning of works by Robbe-Grillet, Simon, Duras, Truffaut, Godard, and Resnais.

Kaplan, A. Y. (1986). *Reproductions of banality: Fascism, literature and French intellectual life.* Minneapolis: University of Minnesota Press.

This is an analysis of the ideology and aesthetics of French fascist writers. Of special interest are the sections on Brasillach, Céline, Drieu la Rochelle, and Rebatet. The book includes an interview with Maurice Bardèche.

Kremer, S. L. (1999). *Women's Holocaust writing: Memory and imagination.* Lincoln: University of Nebraska Press.

This is an excellent work that focuses on American Holocaust literature by women and on representations of women's Holocaust experiences.

Langer, L. L. (1978). *The age of atrocity: Death in modern literature.* Boston: Beacon Press.

Examining, among others, the works of Thomas Mann, Albert Camus, Alexander Solzhenitzyn, and Charlotte Delbo, Langer explores the evolution of the idea of atrocity in the 20th century and its impact on our notions of the human image. His last chapter on Delbo concentrates on her "frozen" images of the body and the physicality of death and dying, images that denote the corruptive power of atrocity and leave little room for notions of transcendent longing or redemptive insight.

Marks, E. (1996). *Marrano as metaphor: The Jewish presence in French writing.* New York: Columbia University Press.

This work offers a comprehensive analysis of the Jewish involvement in French literature from the 16th century to contemporary times.

Morris, A. (1992). *Collaboration and Resistance reviewed: Writers and the "mode retro" in post-Gaullist France.* Oxford: Berg International.

Morris' work is the first full-length examination of the reappraisal of the Occupation that was known as the "mode retro" and occurred in French writing of the 1970s and 1980s. The author presents the legacy of the Occupation in its cultural and historical context and gives reasons for the development of the

"mode retro." He focuses on a generation of writers who, having had collabo-
rating fathers, attempt to create in their works alternative myths of the
Occupation and collaboration. He looks particularly at the works of Pascal
Jardin, Evelyne Le Garrec, Marie Chaix, and Patrick Modiano.

Suleiman, S. R. (1994). *Risking who one is: Encounters with contemporary art
and literature.* Cambridge: Harvard University Press.

In this wonderful collection of essays, two are particularly noteworthy: (1)
"Life-Story, History, Fiction: Simone de Beauvoir's Wartime Writings" discusses the changing image of Beauvoir with the 1990 publication of her war
diaries. It also offers a new reading of her novel about the war, *Le Sang des
autres,* published in 1945. (2) "War Memories: On Autobiographical Reading" is a study primarily of memoirs by Jews who were children during the
war (Saul Friedlander, Georges Perec, Elie Wiesel, and Claudine Vegh). It
defines autobiographical reading as "reading another person's story as if it
were your own."

Weitz, M. C. (1995). *Sisters in the Resistance: How women fought to free France,
1940-1945.* New York: J. Wiley.

Weitz's work, dedicated "to all the French women who resisted occupation,
oppression, and injustice," interestingly portrays the courage and strength of
French women at all levels. From Lucie Aubrac to the women who trans-
ported coded information or even ammunitions in their bicycle baskets or
baby carriages, Weitz tells their stories with candor and historical accuracy.
Weitz also includes examples of stories of women who collaborated with the
Nazi occupiers. In 1994 Weitz edited a special journal issue on the same topic:
Mémoire et oubli: Women of the French Resistance. *Contemporary French
Civilization, 18* (1).

## IV. CLASSROOM ACTIVITIES AND PROJECTS

I recommend that a teaching unit on the Holocaust and the events of World
War II begin with short documentaries (in videotape or audiocassette format) of
survivor testimony (e.g., *Visages de la Shoah*), to be followed by published memoirs of survivors. Building upon this base of knowledge, proceed with feature-length
films accompanied by script scenarios (e.g., *Le Dernier métro, Au revoir les enfants*,
or *Lacombe Lucien*). Complement these exercises with the study of literary works
based on Vichy France.

What follows is a list of possible student-centered activities that allow for
independent reflection on the part of the student. An important goal of all these
activities, beyond the expansion of foreign language skills, is to remember the
Holocaust and to develop tolerance for the differences perceived in others.

1.  **Invite guest speakers (e.g., local Holocaust survivors or former hidden children). Contact the nearest Holocaust Resource Center for suggestions.**
    Students respond exceedingly well to interaction with a Holocaust survivor or hidden child. Students who have been sensitized to the horrors of the Holocaust and World War II are extremely conscious of the need to ask respectful and content-appropriate questions. This activity greatly enhances foreign language skills because students are motivated by the interaction with an actual survivor.

2.  **Have students write letters (in the target language) to survivors or former hidden children.**
    Like Activity #1, students pay close attention to their writing skills as they do not want to offend the Holocaust survivor or hidden child. Moreover, when students receive a written response, they are deeply moved.

3.  **Plan creative responses to the study of the Holocaust (e.g., poems, art work, or essays).**
    As an extension of Activities #1 and #2, ask students to express in a creative form of their own choosing what they have learned or experienced. A suggested follow-up to this activity is to have students present their projects to their fellow classmates.

4.  **Develop creative responses to Holocaust or Occupation literature. Ask students to write a letter (in the target language) to a literary character or characters.**
    This is similar to Activity #2 but this time is inspired by literature. Using "Le Silence de la mer" by Vercors, for example, give the following assignment: "You are Werner von Ebrennac. Write a letter to the uncle and the niece in which you describe the time you spent quartered in their house, mentioning your feelings about the war and the way you were received in their home."

5.  **Focus on the events of World War II from a cross-cultural perspective.**
    Using *Dr. Seuss Goes to War: The World War II Editorial Cartoons of Theodor Seuss Geisel* by Richard H. Minear, have students compare American editorial cartoons with Nazi propaganda posters (available, for example, from the U.S. Holocaust Memorial Museum in Washington, D.C.) or with the brief cartoon depiction of American bomber pilots in Chabrol's documentary film, *L'Oeil de Vichy* (q.v.).

6.  **Attend an art exhibition or a theater production.**
    Many art museums, galleries, and theaters present works on the Holocaust.

7.  **If possible, visit the U.S. Holocaust Memorial Museum in Washington, DC, or the Museum of Tolerance in Los Angeles.**
    A visit to these excellent museums is a wonderful opportunity for students and teachers alike. The exhibits, resource centers, and computer displays are excellent. If financial constraints or time and distance prohibit a visit, contact the nearest Holocaust Resource Center for a list of activities and exhibits in your area.

8. **Develop Internet projects using Web sites dealing with the Holocaust.**
   The Internet provides a wealth of opportunities for student projects related to the Holocaust and World War II. Encourage students to explore on their own, especially with French search engines such as <http://www.wanadoo.fr>. The U.S. Holocaust Memorial Museum maintains an outstanding Web site and is a highly recommended classroom tool. Warning: As with all Internet activities, sites need to be monitored for accuracy and assessability. There is a great deal of Holocaust denial on the Internet.

9. **Have students give oral presentations using video clips from films and documentaries.**
   Following the traditional form of an *explication de texte* of a literary work, students can do an oral presentation based on a clip from a film or a documentary. Let students explore what is available from their local or school libraries or, if possible, download real audio from the Internet. Students take great pride in discovering and explaining materials that they themselves find.

10. **Present television broadcasts (France 2) and documentaires dealing with Vichy France and the Holocaust. Be sure to highlight current events in the news.**
    Much is in the news lately about Vichy France (e.g., the trials of Maurice Papon, racist attitudes in Switzerland and France, insurance claims by Holocaust survivors, and the Papal apology). Current events are a rich source for classroom discussion and must not be overlooked. Studying current events also emphasizes that the Holocaust and World War II are not ancient history and have great bearing on how we conduct our lives today. A better understanding of history as well as current events may teach us how to protect future generations from similar horrors. Discussion can be expanded to draw parallels, for example, to the events in Kosovo.

# 8
# Teaching for Tolerance: Community-Based Learning for the Spanish Classroom

**Ruth Kauffmann**
William Jewell College

## Responding to New Curricular Directives

As we enter the 21st century, educators are being increasingly asked to engage students in the learning process. Traditional lectures have given way to more interactive techniques such as role-playing, group activities, and discussions. We have become aware that learning a language involves learning about the cultures that use the language, so our textbooks now include more readings about people and places. Students are introduced to cultural differences concerning family, work, meal schedules, and educational systems, for example. Yet even as sources of information are becoming ever more sophisticated with the Internet and on-line periodicals and newspapers, there is a growing awareness that knowledge about cultures may not be enough to promote tolerance, understanding, and communication between cultures.

The *Standards for Foreign Language Learning in the 21st Century* (National Standards in Foreign Language Education Project, 1999) emphasize this new understanding of the way cultural learning takes place:

> The enduring dimension of cultural study is the actual participation in the exchange of information and ideas among members of various cultures using the foreign language. While a great deal of information about other cultures can be gained through the study of other disciplines, such as the social sciences and the arts, only second language study empowers learners to engage successfully in meaningful, direct interaction, both orally and in writing, with members of other cultures. The perspectives, practices, and products of culture—be they historical or contemporary—can be shared in a special way with members of the culture in which they originated. This new, "insider's" perspective is the true catalyst for cross-cultural understanding (p. 49).

This call for "meaningful, direct interaction" is at best difficult to meet within the confines of the classroom. Since language provides a unique skill, i.e., the ability to communicate with people from outside our own culture, we as language teachers should use this advantage to its fullest potential. In the U.S. today, opportunities to practice Spanish with Spanish-speaking community groups can provide students the cultural competencies they may never be able to develop in the classroom setting alone.

The *Missouri Foreign Language Standards* (Missouri State Foreign Language Standards Project, 2001) were modeled on the national *Standards* and also include competencies in 5 areas–Communication, Cultures, Connections, Comparisons, and Communities. These "Show-Me" standards affirm that as students learn about culture, they will not simply acquire information but will also be able to recognize distinctive viewpoints. They are expected to engage in conversations using the target language and to use the language both within and beyond the school setting. Students are asked to demonstrate an understanding of the relationship between the practices and the perspectives of the culture studied and to compare the foreign culture with their own, an ability that implies an understanding of themselves as cultural entities.

These new standards grow out of an acknowledgment that teaching must truly engage students. The process of learning a new language includes an initiation into the culture or cultures that use that language. Often this can be an uncomfortable process, as the assumptions of these cultures may come into conflict with the student's own cultural conditioning. Bean (1996) sees this as an opportunity for intellectual growth and development of critical thinking skills: "A good way to foster such reflection is to undermine students' confidence in their own settled beliefs or assumptions by creating what psychologists call cognitive dissonance" (p. 27). The questions and doubts raised by this conflict create the *cognitive dissonance* for our students, and while this is not the primary goal of cultural education, it provides the teacher an opportunity to stimulate dialogue and undermine assumptions that may inhibit intellectual and social growth in the students.

Because languages are intimately bound to their cultures, language professionals have long valued the role of multicultural education in the process of second language acquisition. As Goodlad (1986) has stated,

> Multiculturalism must be seen to embrace the whole of humankind. From a strategic point of view, this maturing of multicultural education through cooperative pluralism represents an opportunity of joining with other groups and other movements designed to assist the human race to live together in understanding, appreciation, and peace.

Tiedt and Tiedt (1990) propose a rationale for multicultural education that is summarized as follows:

- We are individuals who have an identity that is shaped in part by our culture.
- Cultural awareness is the first step toward the ability to engage other cultures.

- Education should dispel ignorance and promote racial and global harmony. (pp. 3-5)

Nieto (1992) theorizes that through a program of multicultural education, as students learn about themselves and others, they will be moved along a continuum of understanding, from tolerance to acceptance to respect, and finally to affirmation, solidarity, and critique.

Early programs of multicultural education very often omitted any experiences and activities outside of the classroom. Sometimes they were designed for classrooms with students from diverse social, cultural, and racial backgrounds, and sometimes they simply assumed that interactive and engaging classroom activities would be sufficient to move students along the desired continuum, from ignorance and fear of those who are different from themselves, to affirmation and understanding of those differences.

In 1938 John Dewey pointed to the need for experience as the basis for all learning. Nostrand (1966) confirmed that personal interaction is essential to language learning, asserting that no matter how technically dexterous a student's training in the foreign language, that training would be of no value without direct contact with native speakers of the target language. Technical training, without respect for a cultural world view, has little value (pp. 5-8).

Hale (1999) writes that educators and social activists like Dewey, Gandhi, Freire, and Giroux contend that education should be based on serving the community and not simply on acquiring a body of information. Higher learning that includes a call to altruistic service can then be an agent of social transformation. It is this shift from an emphasis on information-gathering to a goal of social awareness through interactive experience that is being called for in education today.

## Expanding Goals for Language Acquisition

Krashen (1982) makes a distinction between language acquisition and language learning. *Acquisition* is a subconscious process that occurs as we try to communicate, while the more conscious *learning* happens as rules are taught and applied in a systematic and artificial classroom environment. According to Krashen's theory, the internalization of the language happens as the learner starts to communicate using language that he or she knows and through a process of trial and error begins to be able to apply knowledge about the language to actual communicative tasks. Brown (1994) confirms that appropriate and meaningful communication in the second language is the best possible practice.

The current application of acquisition theory to the communicative approach used in most foreign language classrooms today supports the idea that language practice should begin to move out of the classroom and into the community. For teachers who have access to non-anglophone communities in their own geographical areas, the possibility of connecting students to this resource should be taken seriously. In my experience, simply providing events for students to attend did not encourage engagement and interactions with native speakers of Spanish. Consequently, I began to look at models for community-based learning that had been established by other foreign language teachers.

Varas (1999) engaged her students at Willamette University in a community outreach program that paired her students with elementary school students enrolled in the Migrant Education Program. She discovered that the two hours each week that her students spent with the Spanish-speaking children motivated the students in their language studies and provided practice at each student's skill level through the interactive learning context of the pairing. In addition, her students developed cross-cultural skills and became more sensitive to cultural and class differences. This awareness addressed deeper issues of prejudice, intolerance, and racism. She also found that her students gained confidence and leadership skills and gave the best of themselves to the program. She integrated her Service Learning Unit into the classroom with texts, discussions, and assignments. Students in her classroom gave presentations on their experiences, read texts that helped them gain knowledge about the community of people with whom they were working, and wrote papers that reflected on the culture and lives of these children.

Boyle and Overfield (1999) take the idea of service learning one step further by advocating "community-based learning." They feel that this term underscores the fact that all participants in the cross-cultural exchange are co-constructors of the learning experience. For them, the new term erases the sense of superiority that the "helper" may feel over the person or group receiving a service and emphasizes the cooperative nature of the learning taking place. Taking the learning process outside of the classroom provides yet another opportunity to remove boundaries and barriers between social and racial groups.

## Service-Learning at William Jewell College

In my own classroom, an awareness of the need for true interaction between my students and the Spanish-speaking cultures inspired me in 1997 to institute a *Cultural Series* in all my language classes. I developed a list (series) of a variety of opportunities for students to interact with Hispanics, both on campus and throughout the Kansas City metropolitan area. This series included movies, artistic and dance events, museum exhibits, conversations with native speakers, and festivals and holiday celebrations such as El Día de los Muertos and El Cinco de Mayo. Each student was asked to attend two events and write a short summary and evaluation of each experience.

The cultural series represented 5% of the student's grade for the course. The response to this requirement was generally positive, and most students reported having fun completing the series. Overall, the students reported that the events were very helpful in understanding Hispanic cultures and made it easier to understand the Spanish language. They appreciated the chance to see the culture in "real life." However, some expressed frustration that there was not enough free time to complete the series and that too much of the grade was based on attendance at these events. The addition of a service-learning component as an optional unit in my Intermediate Spanish I class was an effort to extend the learning that the cultural series had afforded the students and give them the opportunity to have personal interactions with people in a Spanish-speaking community. I was also struggling to find ways to develop true cultural competencies.

My efforts to provide a service-learning component in my Intermediate I Spanish  class have been supported by the Service Learning Program at Jewell. Through this program, students at Jewell document their volunteer hours on their transcripts. The institution officially values their volunteer service, and students can point to this record for reference by future employers and graduate schools. In addition, the service learning coordinator has provided my class with van transportation and funds when necessary. In the fall of 2000, I first offered a *Service Learning Unit* (SLU) as an optional part of the Intermediate Class. Students who chose this option were required to volunteer 15 hours during the semester at one of the agencies or schools in the Kansas City area that service a Spanish-speaking population. At the conclusion of these hours, students were to write a two-page reflective paper in Spanish on that experience.

Of the 21 students enrolled in my class, 14 opted to complete the SLU by performing their volunteer services at various agencies:

**Shalom House**. Students prepared an evening meal and shared in the meal and conversation with residents of this temporary shelter for homeless men operated by the Maryknoll Catholic Volunteers. About 60% of the men served there are Spanish-speaking.

**Mattie Rhodes Art Gallery**. Students assisted with creative projects in this gallery and got to know the children and their art instructors. The gallery provides after-school art activities for children from the Primitivo García Magnet School across the street. About 95% of these children are of Mexican origin.

**El Centro English as a Second Language Program**. Students served as tutors for the adults and assisted with English instruction in this center that provides many services to the Hispanic population of the Argentine District of Kansas City, Kansas.

**Amnesty International**. Students reviewed cases listed on the Amnesty International Web site and wrote letters in Spanish on behalf of people who had suffered human rights violations in Spanish-speaking countries. First they reviewed several cases and selected a particular one to address. These were very time-consuming projects since the letters required many rewrites, but the two students who chose to write these letters became acutely aware of human rights abuses around the world.

Students who completed the SLU were overwhelmingly positive about their experiences. Of course they were delighted not to take the final exam, which the SLU replaced. The personal gains that they reported were remarkable:

- *Students became aware of the struggles of new immigrants to the United States*: "I came to appreciate the strong desire that these students had to learn English. For them, English wasn't just another language, but a necessary language. They need to know English in order to be able to survive and function in the United States."

- *Personal conversations helped break down class and racial differences*: "At Shalom House, I talked to a shy man named Carlos from Colombia. He showed me pictures of his two children. He was only able to go home to visit at Christmas and was sad that he could see his family only once a year. Carlos made me realize that not too many of us talk to immigrants as if they were just regular people and that he appreciated it that I would treat him with kindness and respect."

- *Students were able to witness others working selflessly*: "My favorite thing about Shalom House was the director, Mary, [...] an older woman who has dedicated her life to noble ideals. She helps these men, attends conferences, and raises money for a variety of projects. I hope that one day I can be like her."

- *Students were motivated to improve their Spanish*: "At the Mattie Rhodes Art Gallery almost all of the children were bilingual in English and Spanish. I realized that all Americans should learn languages other than English. I think that this is very important for the future of the culture of the United States. Children who are able to learn more languages have a great advantage."

- *Students gained a heightened sense of the importance of volunteering*: "It's easy to forget others when we get busy with our own lives. Because of the requirements for the Service Project, I was reminded that our goal in life should be to help others in need."

The students all agreed that the amount of time they had put into the SLU was far greater than the time they would have spent studying for the final examination. When I asked them if they would do it again if they had the choice, they unanimously agreed that they would. They affirmed that the contact with Spanish speakers during their service hours challenged them to use what they knew and made the classroom experience even more meaningful. They expressed a new appreciation for the Spanish-speaking communities in Kansas City and a desire to continue learning Spanish after the completion of the course.

## Some Guidelines and Suggestions for Community-Based Learning Units

In order to get the most out of experiential learning, the teacher must provide programmatic opportunities for reflection and discussion. Hale (1999) suggests a cycle of *experience*, which leads to *reflective thinking* and produces *learning*, which is then applied to the next *experience* (p. 16). Varona (1999) suggests that the student start with interpretation of a new situation and then interact with the people in their assignment, gaining critical knowledge through the process of evaluation and reflection that can then be applied to their efforts to interpret the world around them. For Varona, it is this process that leads to true understanding and the ability to see the world from another's point of view. Smith (1999) observed that her students gained clarity and insight as they left what was familiar to venture into new social contexts. At William Jewell College, I saw in my own students a new curiosity about the world and a willingness to explore career options that they may not have considered before, e.g. the Peace Corps or Teach For America.

## Some Challenges

Those who have tried to incorporate community-based experiences into the classroom share similar frustrations, some of which I can confirm with my own experience. These include:

- **Scheduling.** Many of our students have scheduling issues because they have jobs or are involved in extracurricular campus activities. For them to be able to coordinate their schedules with the agency they are serving can be difficult if not impossible. Several of my students who play inter-collegiate sports have opted not to complete the SLU because of their schedules.

- **Time Commitment.** Faculty time invested in coordinating students and agencies, setting up potential assignments, or making community visits is usually in addition to an already overburdened workload. I have found, however, that much of this work can be done over the telephone or by e-mail from my office, and once an agency has worked with student volunteers it is usually eager to have more students come.

- **Bureaucracy.** Difficulties often arise in matching agency needs with student capabilities and schedules. In some cases, the process of becoming a volunteer involves extensive paper work and several hours of training. Most students find these obstacles insurmountable. I have opted to connect students with agencies that require little in the way of preparatory training and documentation.

- **Transportation.** If your institution is located at a distance from the Spanish-speaking communities in your area, transportation may become a problem. Students will need to have their own transportation unless you plan to provide transportation through program funds. My students typically travel 20 or 30 minutes to their volunteer assignments. For some students, especially those who do not have a car, this consideration may be a factor in deciding whether or not to participate in the SLU.

- **Assessment.** Perhaps the biggest challenge for the educator is to rethink the process of evaluation. Traditionally, grades in foreign language courses have been based on learning skill sets related to grammar and writing skills. In a Spanish course that values cultural awareness, the process of evaluation must somehow reflect that value.

In my Intermediate I Spanish class, I have replaced the 15% of the grade once earned through the final exam with the Service Learning Unit. In the SLU, the grade is determined by the documented completion of 15 volunteer hours and a two-page reflection paper in Spanish. My reasoning is that the experience using the language in a real cultural setting has moved the students further along the path toward acquisition of language skills than a single exam could ever do. (Students still have 40% of their grade based on seven chapter exams.) I am not satisfied with this elective approach, as I think it does not truly make the SLU an integral part of the course. I would like to create an intermediate course that would integrate the cultural experience more fully into the rest of the class. The curriculum itself should include interactions with native speakers and involvement with local Spanish-speaking communities as a part of the evaluated classroom experience.

I believe that the *Standards* have correctly identified the need for real cultural interaction in acquiring cultural competency. We as language teachers should accept the challenge of creating curricula and activities that address this need and explore options that will be viable and assessable. We especially need to think about how students can acquire cultural competencies in classrooms, even without the proximity of Spanish-speaking communities. In the meantime, we need to begin to use to the fullest extent possible the resources that are available to us and to include cultural competencies in our list of objectives for our Spanish classrooms.

## References

Bean, J. C. (1996). *Engaging ideas.* San Francisco: Jossey-Bass Publishers.

Boyle, J. P. & Overfield, D. M. (1999). Community-based language learning: Integrating language and service. In J. Hellebrandt & L. Varona (Eds.), *Construyendo puentes (Building bridges): Concepts and models for service-learning in Spanish* (pp. 137-148). Washington, DC: American Association for Higher Education.

Brown, H. D. (1994). *Principles of language learning and teaching* (3rd ed.). Englewood Cliffs, NJ: Prentice Hall Regents.

Goodlad, J. I. (1986). Speech given at the Center for Educational Renewal. Seattle: University of Washington.

Hale, A. (1999). Service learning and Spanish: A missing link. In J. Hellebrandt & L. Varona (Eds.), *Construyendo puentes (Building bridges): Concepts and models for service-learning in Spanish* (pp. 9-32). Washington, DC: American Association for Higher Education.

Krashen, S. (1982). *Principles and practice in second language acquisition*. New York: Pergamon Press.

Missouri State Foreign Language Standards Project. (2001). *Missouri foreign language standards*, D. Bachman (Ed.). Jefferson City: Missouri Department of Elementary and Secondary Education.

National Standards in Foreign Language Education Project. (1999). *Standards for foreign langue learning in the 21st century*. Lawrence, KS: Allen Press.

Nieto, S. (1992). *Affirming diversity: The sociopolitical context of multicultural education*. New York: Longman Publishing Group.

Nostrand, H. (1966). Describing and teaching the sociocultural context of a foreign language and literature. In Valdman, A. (Ed.), *Trends in language teaching* (pp. 1-25). New York: McGraw-Hill.

Smith, N. J. (1999). Expanding our vision of literacy: Learning to read the world of others. In J. Hellebrandt & L. Varona (Eds.), *Construyendo puentes (Building bridges): Concepts and models for service-learning in Spanish* (pp. 171-196). Washington, DC: American Association for Higher Education.

Tiedt, P. & Tiedt, I. M. (1990). *Multicultural teaching*. (3rd. ed.). Boston: Allyn and Bacon Press.

Varas, P. (1999). Raising cultural awareness through service-learning in Spanish culture and conversation: Tutoring in the migrant education program in Salem. In J. Hellebrandt & L. Varona (Eds.), *Construyendo puentes (Building bridges): Concepts and models for service-learning in Spanish* (pp. 123-136). Washington, DC: American Association for Higher Education.

Varona, L. (1999). From instrumental to interactive to critical knowledge through service-learning in Spanish. In J. Hellebrandt & L. Varona (Eds.), *Construyendo puentes (Building bridges): Concepts and models for service-learning in Spanish* (pp. 61-77). Washington, DC: American Association for Higher Education.

# 9

# Experiential Education Abroad: Service-Learning, Project-Based Learning, and Internships in Germany

**Jefford Vahlbusch**
University of Wisconsin-Eau Claire

In the recently published *Higher Education Service-Learning Sourcebook*, Robin J. Crews states that although "most service-learning occurs in [...] the United States, *international* service-learning has been around for a long time and is gaining in visibility and popularity today" (2002, p. 26). This is true in large part because of the excellent programs offered by organizations cited by Crews, for example the International Partnership for Service-Learning, the School for International Training in Brattleboro, Vermont, and the UK Centres for Experiential Learning (p. 26). Nonetheless, these gains in visibility and popularity, although encouraging, cannot yet be characterized as broadly significant. While the practice of service-learning abroad is certainly increasing, the available evaluative and scholarly literature–and therefore the quality of reflection on international service-learning–does not seem to be keeping pace. Neither the printed nor the electronic literatures and other resources on service-learning in the United States offer sufficiently detailed and practical help to those who might wish to develop service-learning opportunities abroad. This seems to hold even if service-learning abroad is defined loosely enough to include certain kinds of international service-only programs and internships, as Crews appears willing to allow (p. 26). Although there are welcome and helpful exceptions to be found–especially in the superb, pioneering work of Chisholm and Berry (1992, 1999) and Chisholm (2000)–establishing and conducting a service-learning program or experience abroad is itself still a matter of experiential education. Although this will always remain true to some extent because of the uniqueness of each service-learner and each placement, the particular problems, challenges, and benefits of international service-learning are still in need of much study and articulation.

Not surprisingly, the amount of available scholarship and other helpful guidance diminishes even further if the service-learning in question is to be performed completely, mostly, or even partly in a language other than English. Although excellent international service-learning opportunities in languages other than English certainly do exist (and have existed for some time), they also have received far less publicity and critical attention than they need and deserve.[1] Excellent research and publicity work has been done on service-learning and experiential education undertaken by students in Hispanic communities throughout the United States; some research and descriptive work has been done on service-learning programs in Mexico and Latin America as well. As one might expect, much of this work also presents useful lessons about the theory and the practice of service-learning that might be conducted in other languages and other cultures abroad.[2] We clearly need more than this, and more than can be learned from the occasional syllabus or course description posted on-line. What we need at this stage are practical descriptions of service-learning and other experiential learning opportunities that are currently being offered in foreign-language-based study-abroad programs by colleges and universities in the United States. It is in such programs that much future growth in international service-learning will and should come. People and institutions will be looking in this area for generally applicable answers about service-learning and service-learning abroad and for country-specific and language-specific advice.

Service-learning is, of course, not just service; in its simplest definition, it involves "community service in conjunction with guided reflection" (Ehrlich, 1996, p. xiii). At its best, service-learning offers students the "opportunity to enrich and apply classroom knowledge; explore careers or majors; develop civic and cultural literacy; improve citizenship; develop occupational skills; enhance personal growth and self-image; establish job links; and foster a concern for social problems" (Brevard Community College, 1994). According to Eyler and Giles (1999), those who participate in service-learning tend to realize a number of valuable experiences or achievements:

- a reduction of negative stereotypes and an increase in tolerance for diversity;
- greater self-knowledge;
- greater spiritual growth;
- increased ability to work with others;
- increased leadership skills;
- increased feeling of being connected to a community;
- increased connection to the college experience through closer ties to students and faculty;
- increased reported learning and motivation to learn;
- deeper understanding of subject matter;
- deeper understanding of the complexity of social issues;
- increased ability to apply material learned in class to real problems (quoted as summarized in: <www.compact.org/resource/s-lbrochuredefinitions.html>.

If we imagine that even some of this can be attained by students using a foreign language in a foreign society and culture, then the potential power of
service-learning abroad and its particular benefits for our language students and
our programs begin to become clear. Service-learning abroad in a foreign language can build linguistic, cultural, and civic competence; can engage our students
in the challenge of personal growth through service; and can offer them the sort of
personal involvement and investment in their new communities and languages
that few study-abroad programs can guarantee. As Crews puts it in more general
terms, international service-learning programs can add "global literacy and citizenship, multicultural education and experience, and international
community-building to the mix of benefits in service-learning's already impressive portfolio" (2002, p. 26).

**The Wittenberg Program**

The University of Wisconsin-Eau Claire's study-abroad program in
Wittenberg, Germany, in outline, seems quite traditional. Students in any field
from any college or university who have completed at least the third (and prefer-
ably the fourth) semester of college-level German can spend 14 weeks, from late
January to the end of April, studying German language, culture, literature, history,
and contemporary life at the Institut für deutsche Sprache und Kultur in Wittenberg.[3]
This Institut, our partner in the program, is an independent affiliate of the vener-
able University of Halle-Wittenberg that specializes in custom-designing and
administering language and culture programs in Germany for foreign students.
During their time in Wittenberg, our students live individually with German host
families, undertake a number of important guided excursions in the region, participate in quite a wide variety of cultural, social, academic, and athletic activities,
and enjoy ample time for studying, socializing, and traveling. All instruction and
all student work are in German. One of the four faculty members in our German
program at the university accompanies and directs the program (on a rotating basis) and teaches two courses. In 1999 and again in 2000, 14 students took part. In
2001, 20 students completed the program, and 23 are participating in 2002.

Since 1995, the University of Wisconsin-Eau Claire has been the only member of the University of Wisconsin system and one of the few public universities
of any size in the country to require that its candidates for the baccalaureate degree
complete a major service-learning project.[4] According to the university's *Service-
Learning Guidebook*, these 30 mandated hours of experiential learning are intended
"to provide students with opportunities to serve their community, to apply knowledge gained in the classroom, and to enhance their critical thinking skills" (2001,
p. 1). In recent years, the university has also gained a reputation as an institution
committed to study abroad. With the help of our Center for International Education, a large number of our students study abroad each year. Measured as a
percentage of degree completions–one of the two calculation methods employed
as industry standards by the Institute for International Education in New York

City–the 333 Eau Claire students who engaged in some sort of study-abroad experience in Academic Year 1999-2000 represented a nearly 24% participation rate. In the same year, the university ranked 16th in the nation when its study-abroad numbers were compared with those of similar institutions (Institute for International Education, 2001). Given these twin emphases of service-learning and study abroad, it is not surprising that in 1999, when the Wittenberg program was founded, the decision was made to offer program participants the chance to fulfill their service-learning requirement while in Germany. This initial decision has had important positive effects and has also helped lead to other significant developments. Within its traditional structure and curriculum, the Wittenberg program now offers its students a closely woven net of project- and community-based learning, service-learning experiences, and optional short-term internships in business and the professions.

**Experiential Education in Wittenberg**

*Project-Based Learning.* Much of the teaching and learning in the program is itself experiential in nature, i.e., task- and project-based. The teaching and learning has always involved extensive student work within the Wittenberg community and intensive student interaction with the citizens of Wittenberg. Through these interactions students have learned about the city's history, its citizens, and the past and present problems of the city and its region. Wittenberg, still best known as the place where Martin Luther started the Protestant Reformation, is located on the Elbe River about 120 kilometers south of Berlin in the former East Germany and is now a city with a population of just under 50,000.

Issues addressed during a Wittenberg semester might easily range from aspects of Martin Luther's theology or his political views, to the work and the victims of the "State Security" organization or *Stasi*, to the entrepreneurial successes and failures in Wittenberg after the dissolution of East Germany in 1989. During the 2001 program, for example, our students spent two weeks interviewing, fact-checking, discussing, researching, debating, and writing on aspects of the troubled environmental history of the region that is now the federal German state of Sachsen-Anhalt. This work concluded with presentations to their fellow students. Some focused on ongoing private and government initiatives to detoxify, reclaim, and find creative ways to use the region's infamous East-German era lignite coal strip mines. Others worked on the then current and divisive proposals to expand commercial and industrial barge traffic on the newly cleaned-up Elbe river, proposals that would involve, among other controversial things, widening and dredging sections of the river, with probable deleterious effects on the river's ecology and the surrounding rich wetlands. Students taking part in these projects had the chance to interact with citizens' groups, individual environmentalists, scientists, the river police, government officials, and officials of the chemical and fertilizer factory, SKW Piesteritz, which is still Wittenberg's largest employer and the owner of the single industrial harbor on Wittenberg's stretch of the Elbe.

*Service-Learning.* Since our program's inception, each participating student has undertaken a 30-hour individual service-learning project while in Wittenberg. (This includes students who have already completed their service-learning requirement elsewhere, or whose majors–such as education–ask them to complete the requirement in other ways.) Whatever one's opinion about *requiring* students to serve others, if undertaken abroad by students of a foreign language and if properly organized and carried out, such service-learning experiences can be of inestimable value. In service-learning in a foreign language, the linguistic stakes are instantly raised far beyond the levels of interest and seriousness ever attained in the classroom. Each student must use what he or she has learned of the language and the culture to accomplish specific, needed tasks beyond the reach and assumptions of a traditional learning environment. Each student is thereby given the chance to function in the foreign language as an individual with a semi-professional role in the community, and these connections remain distinct from both the study-abroad program group and the host family. Students can thereby become, in a modest way and for a short time, recognized and valued members of their new community, using their often painfully-won knowledge of the language and culture to accomplish something practical, tangible, visible, useful, and good. In the best cases, students find that they suddenly have a new sort of status in the study-abroad group and in their host family and a new sort of stake in the adventure of life abroad. In the best cases, the feelings of belonging and accomplishment that come with successful service are often more intense and more profound than the transitory celebrity conferred by foreignness and often more interesting and more memorable than the pleasures of trophy travel or incidental celluloid tourism.

In Wittenberg since 1999, with the invaluable organizational help and through the rich local contacts of the Institut für deutsche Sprache und Kultur, our students have been able to serve one full day per program week in soup kitchens; in residential homes for the elderly and in nursing homes; in shelters for the homeless; in various sorts of kindergartens, private and public, some of them for children who are cognitively or physically challenged; in social service agencies; in a women's cafe; in a counseling and job-training center for youth; in a school center for gardening and ecology; in the city forest and children's zoo; in city unemployment counseling offices; at the Wittenberg Youth Hostel; in various elementary schools; in an art school for children; in a hospital emergency room; or in a substance-abuse treatment and counseling center. Where these service-learning placements and experiences have been successful, our students have ranked them at or near the top of their lists of best and most meaningful experiences in Germany and in our Wittenberg program. In program evaluations and informal exit interviews, most students responded that they had gained personally and linguistically from their service, and many also wished that they could have spent more time with the people and the agency they served.

*Short-term Internships.* In the 2001 program year, we added a short-term unpaid business-and-professional-internship option to the program. For an additional $675, which includes Institut tuition fees, room, and board, students may now choose to extend their stay in Wittenberg for an additional four weeks in order to serve full-time in one to four local firms, offices, factories, or agencies. We ask that students select a focus for their internships–such as law, advertising, or city planning–in consultation with the program's resident director and the staff of the Institut, and we support students with on-site faculty mentoring and at least four hours of instruction per week in business etiquette, business practices, and business German. Both students who participated in our 2001 pilot program did so, in part at least, to explore possible careers, and both asked for the greatest possible variety of placements. One chose to focus on advertising and marketing. She spent time working and shadowing in a large agency charged with marketing the city of Wittenberg; in a one-person advertising firm specializing in small businesses; in a Lutheran educational foundation that organizes religious and cultural events in the region; and in the sales and marketing department of a major producer of heavy milling equipment. The other student chose architecture and construction and was able to work as an intern in both the largest and the smallest construction firms in Wittenberg; in the city's urban-planning office; and with a construction foreman overseeing building projects from Berlin to Leipzig. (For this last position, the student had to provide sturdy clothing, gloves, and work boots, but she was formally presented with her very own hardhat on day one.) In their exit interviews, both students reported that dressing, acting, and working as members of the regular workforce in Wittenberg had given them a new sense of self and purpose. Both felt that their understanding of everyday life in Germany deepened during the internship month and that their German language abilities improved. Both felt that their knowledge of the economic and social realities of Wittenberg and Sachsen-Anhalt grew immensely. Both of them were also delighted that after-work socializing with German co-workers became a regular event. Interestingly, the student who focused on advertising and marketing learned during the internship that she might rather spend her work-life in other pursuits.

## Experiential Education and the Major in German

At the end of September 2001, the German program at the University of Wisconsin-Eau Claire had 44 declared majors and 35 declared minors in German. Like most advanced language students currently enrolled at universities and colleges across the country, all of these German majors have another major. Most of them in fact consider this "other" major to be their primary major, the course of study and the vocational orientation that they hope or believe will form the foundation for their careers and their lives. Like our minors, our majors today therefore typically see the in-depth study of German (including their study abroad) as a gateway or path, as a practical means to professional and personal goals, and not as an end in itself. A few students, mostly those who are planning to teach, do see German as their primary major; a few see it only as a diversion from "more practical" intellectual or vocational pursuits. Most of our students have excellent reasons for joining German to their "first" major. They want our program to help them to develop competencies and proficiencies in German language, culture, and society that will–among other things–give them good professional experience in their chosen primary fields. Students in the 2001 and 2002 Wittenberg programs represented an extensive and varied list of "other" majors ranging from mathematics, elementary or secondary education, finance, and psychology, to business management, philosophy, religion, technical writing, and forensic science.

None of this is bad news; the study of German is thriving at UW-Eau Claire. These developments do, however, have important implications for our mission and our work. Our challenge has been to find ways truly to serve the professional and vocational needs of our particular students while maintaining our German program as a place to study language, culture, literature, and history in all the depth, breadth, and intensity that must characterize a good undergraduate major. While we affirm and continue to sharpen our focus on language, literature, and culture, we are also interested in developing other significant focal points. Enriching our department's study-abroad program in Wittenberg with project-based instruction, business and professional internships, and especially service-learning has helped us to meet our students' professional needs, improve our major program, and branch out in new directions.

## Recommendations

There are a number of widely accepted "Principles of Good Practice" that have been drafted and approved for service-learning programs in the United States. These principles could and should in the years ahead also be examined and revised for use in thinking about and planning service-learning programs abroad. Perhaps the best known are the so-called "Wingspread Principles of Good Practice for Combining Service and Learning" (Mintz & Hesser, 1996, p. 30).[5]

According to these principles, a service-learning program:

1. Engages people in responsible and challenging actions for the common good.
2. Provides structured opportunities for people to reflect critically on their service experience.
3. Articulates clear service and learning goals for everyone involved.
4. Allows for those with needs to define those needs.
5. Clarifies the responsibilities of each person and organization involved.
6. Matches service providers and service needs through a process that recognizes changing circumstances.
7. Expects genuine, active, and sustained organizational commitment.
8. Includes training, supervision, monitoring, support, recognition, and evaluation to meet service and learning goals.
9. Insures that the time commitment for service and learning is flexible, appropriate, and in the best interests of all involved.
10. Is committed to program participation by and with diverse populations.

For our purposes in this short piece, a distillation of these principles is in order. To borrow a line from a Berea College report whose main author was philosopher Robert Hoag, "learning through service ought to have integrity both as learning and as service, and ought to strive for excellence both as learning and as service" (1998, p. 23). This admonition has a special force and is especially difficult to uphold in service-learning experiences that are conducted abroad in a foreign language and culture. To be successful in our international service-learning programs, we need to find ways to ensure that the work performed by our students during their service-learning projects is truly service as we define it. The work must also respect cultural norms, assumptions, and practices that may differ from our own. We need to find ways to support our students' language-learning during their service-learning and ways to ensure that the goal of learning through service can be attained. Finally, we need to find ways to guarantee that the service performed and the learning undertaken in our program may improve over time, from week to week and from program year to program year.

**1. *Planning and Preparation*.** The success of each service-learning placement abroad depends on the quality of planning undertaken by the coordinating faculty member with the sponsoring agencies prior to the beginning of student service. In essence, the practices, ideals, and goals of service-learning itself and the desired student learning outcomes must be communicated to and affirmed by agency or organization staff members before the first service-learner begins to serve. It is very important to ensure that each agency has meaningful service work for the student to engage in and that its staff members are willing to help the student do just that. The sponsoring agencies must understand that service-learning is supposed to be mutually beneficial and that the goals are providing service *and* learning through service. In the same way, study-abroad program directors must get to know each of the sponsoring agencies and their mission, cultures, and concerns. These sorts of understandings can be difficult to reach across cultures and, as is sometimes necessary, across borders or oceans. Community-based institutions such as the Institut für deutsche Sprache und Kultur can help, but the same sorts of necessities apply: effective cross-cultural communication is required so that expectations and needs on all sides are attainable and clearly defined in advance.

In the same way, the student must prepare in advance, intellectually and linguistically, for the service-learning experience. If most of the preparation takes place in-country in the foreign language with students at widely varying levels of language proficiency, then sufficient faculty and program time is imperative. Students must have as much time as possible to become fully prepared, both as a group and individually. Much of this preparation has to be tailored to each placement, and much has to be done at or toward the beginning of the program when the students' language skills are often comparatively weak. Nevertheless, the goal must be for students to begin their service with some knowledge of their agency, with some knowledge of the governmental or social network in which this agency is embedded, with a heightened awareness of the cultural differences they are likely to encounter, and with a basic vocabulary for their service. Initial understanding should be enabled so that service, reflection, and learning can all begin right away.[6]

**2. *Engaging and Monitoring*.** Students must be willing to engage themselves fully in both the service and the learning. They should be ready to learn how to serve, not only from the agency staff, but also from those whom they are serving. They need to be or become excellent listeners and active questioners; seekers of linguistic, professional, and personal knowledge; gatherers of facts and evidence; note takers; and dictionary users. They should keep a journal in the foreign language that monitors their service experience, recording comments on services and tasks performed, observations made, facts found, questions raised, questions answered, troubles identified, frustrations felt. If possible, the journal should be scanned each week by the faculty coordinator, who can offer help with language difficulties and with formulating questions. Ideally, the faculty member should give short descriptive, evaluative, and analytical writing assignments that draw on the journal and that may later become a part of it. The faculty coordinator should also visit each agency at least once when the student is present, not to interfere, but with the clearly articulated goal of monitoring both service and learning for excellence.

**3. *Reflection and Evaluation*.** Finally, opportunities for students to engage in a structured and extended reflection on their service and their learning should be provided, ideally flowing from the students' work on their journals and from earlier writing assignments. This final reflection might take the form of presentations, formal writing projects, or both. Honoring the principle of reciprocity, another key concept of service-learning, part of the audience for these student presentations and writing projects would be composed of staff members of the sponsoring agencies and organizations.[7] In this way, the learning engaged in by the students during their service-learning experiences might itself become a kind of service to the agencies.

Service-learning and other sorts of experiential education should be understood as methods to enrich traditional study-abroad programs. As we have seen in Wittenberg, these methods can enhance students' learning and understanding, increase students' commitment, and help build bridges of inquiry, service, work, and friendship from the "island" of the program to the community.[8]

**Notes**

[1]    As one encouraging example, I note that for the 2001 convention of the Modern Language Association, the chair of the MLA Advisory Committee on Foreign Languages and Literatures organized a session on "Experiential Learning in Foreign Languages: Its Role and Effectiveness."

[2]    I especially recommend Hellebrandt and Varona (Eds.), *Construyendo puentes (Building bridges): Concepts and models for service-learning in Spanish*, a volume in the AAHE's Series on Service-Learning in the Disciplines. The entire 18-volume series is a boon to the study and practice of discipline-centered service-learning. See also the limited collection of fine course syllabi offered by the Campus Compact at <www.compact.org/links/syllabi.html>.

[3]    The director of the Institut is Prof. Dr. Ingrid Kuhn of the Martin-Luther University of Halle-Wittenberg; its new managing director is Dr. habil. Regina Richter.

[4]    According to Crews, "fewer than ten percent of the colleges and universities included" in the *Sourcebook's* impressive catalogue of institutions with service-learning programs "require service or service-learning to graduate" (2002, p. 32).

[5]    The Wingspread Principles were originally published in Honnet & Poulsen (1989). I quote them from Mintz et al., p. 30.

[6]    For a brief period of time during orientation, demands on faculty time can be quite heavy. Ideally, of course, study-abroad programs should strive to retain the agencies and organizations at which students have had successful service-learning experiences. This way, over time, the difficult work of agency briefing and student preparation can be streamlined.

[7]    On reciprocity, see Stanton, Giles, & Cruz (1999), p. 3; Mintz et al. (1996), pp. 35-37).

[8]    I would like to thank Professor Donald D. Mowry, Interim Director, Center for Service-Learning, and Dr. Karl Markgraf, Director of the Center for International Education, University of Wisconsin-Eau Claire, for their help with this article. Special thanks also to Dr. Imke Lode, Klaus Hülbrock, and Marita Springsguth, all formerly of the Institut für deutsche Sprache und Kultur in Wittenberg, for their guidance on project-based instruction, service-learning, and internships in Germany.

# References

Berry, H. A. & Chisholm, L. A. (1992). *How to serve & learn abroad effectively: Students tell students*. New York: International Partnership for Service-Learning.

Berry, H. A. & Chisholm, L. A. (1999). *Service-learning in higher education around the world: An initial look*. New York: International Partnership for Service-Learning.

Brevard Community College. (1994, July). *The Power*. As quoted in <csf.colorado.edu/sl/what-is-sl.html>.

Chisholm, L. A. (2000). *Charting a hero's journey*. New York: International Partnership for Service Learning.

Crews, R. J. (2002). *Higher education service-learning sourcebook*. Westport, CT, and London: Oryx Press.

Ehrlich, T. (1996) Foreword. In B. Jacoby & Associates. *Service learning in higher education. Concepts and practices*. San Francisco: Jossey-Bass.

Eyler, J. & Giles, D. E., Jr. (1999). *Where's the learning in service-learning?* San Francisco: Jossey-Bass.

Hellebrandt, J. & Varona, L. T. (Eds.). (1999). *Construyendo puentes (Building bridges): Concepts and models for service-learning in Spanish*. Series on Service-Learning in the Disciplines. Washington, DC: American Association for Higher Education.

Hoag, R. W. (1998). The final report of the team on learning through service. Berea, KY: Berea College. Unpublished internal document. Quoted with permission.

Institute for International Education. (2001). U.S. study-abroad–2001 data tables [On-line]. Available: <http://www.opendoorsweb.org>.

Mintz, S. D. & Hesser, G. W. (1996). Principles of good practice in service-learning. In B. Jacoby & Associates (Eds.), *Service-learning in higher education* (pp. 26-52). San Francisco: Jossey-Bass.

Porter Honnet, E. & Poulsen, S. J. (1989). *Principles of good practice for combining service and learning*. Racine, WI: Johnson Foundation.

Stanton, T. K., Giles, D. E., Jr., & Cruz, N. I. (1999). *Service-learning. A movement's pioneers reflect on its origins, practice, and future*. San Francisco: Jossey-Bass.

University of Wisconsin-Eau Claire. (2001). *Service-learning at the University of Wisconsin-Eau Claire. 2001-02 Guidebook* [On-line]. Available: <http://www.uwec.edu/sl>.

# 10
# Costa Rica for Educators: Lessons from an Intercultural Exchange

**Susan Colville-Hall**
University of Akron

Many unique cultural and linguistic experiences are possible in the Spanish-speaking countries of Central and South America, experiences that can enhance, inform, and increase cultural awareness and cross-cultural understanding between the peoples of the United States and those of the countries south of the border. However, these cultures are not often studied or are totally ignored in school curricula in the United States. Language teachers usually teach "what they know best," which means that Spain and Mexico dominate the curricula as students focus on peninsular and Mexican language, cultures, and literatures. Spain and Mexico are also the destinations of most secondary and post-secondary study and travel-abroad programs. As a result, our Spanish curricula in schools K-12 (and in some universities) equip our students with an unbalanced knowledge of the Spanish-speaking world. When I once mentioned to an acquaintance (a Spanish teacher!) that I had just returned from Costa Rica, the response was, "How was life on the island?" As neighbors of Central and South American countries, we *estadounidenses* need to be better informed.

In professional organizations, we see Spanish teachers who are well prepared in language and literary studies. They are also knowledgeable about some elements of popular culture, but they often lack specific knowledge of socio-economic and geo-political aspects of Hispanic cultures. Sadly, in many districts these teachers develop curricula that reflect a narrow training in linguistics and literary criticism rather than a broader base of the language and cultures as a whole. A participant in a graduate summer seminar confessed that she had never taught her students about Latin America because her preparation was *peninsular*, and her study abroad experience was in Spain. Other teachers have often mentioned that they tend to exclude Latin America from their lessons because they are unfamiliar with its language and cultures. Professional development demands that all Spanish educators reach a better cultural awareness and acquire an in-depth understanding of Central and South America. It was for these reasons that we designed a program in Costa Rica to help educators gain a more holistic view of that country and give them opportunities to increase their linguistic ability. We wanted to create a program that would challenge teachers' stereotypes of Latin American countries so that they, in turn, might help their own students develop a more realistic view of

Central and South America. We proposed a summer seminar to Costa Rica that was funded by the Fulbright Hayes Summer Programs Abroad. This seminar was one step in the process of implanting an area studies component into existing elementary and secondary curricula, and, in doing so, attempting to achieve more balance in the teaching of language and culture.

**Rationale for the Costa Rican Model**

Costa Rica was selected as the ideal site for several reasons:

1.  In-depth knowledge of Costa Rica's culture and socio-economic status can change students' perceptions. According to Gorka and Niesenbaum (2001) who surveyed college students at the beginning of an interdisciplinary course that took place in Costa Rica, many U.S. students think that all Central American countries are "poor," "underdeveloped," "illiterate," filled with "primitive populations," and "run by dictators." It is important to help students change this stereotypical view of Central American cultures because maintaining these negative characteristics can influence students and impede their acquisition of the language (Schumann, 1976a; Schumann, 1976b). Costa Rica, the "little Switzerland" of Central America, serves as a perfect model to erode this stereotype.

2.  Education plays an exceptionally important role in the life of Costa Rican people, who claim a "93% literacy rate in those 10 and older" and "pride themselves on having more teachers than policemen" (Baker, 1999, p. 96). Several facts can be enumerated to demonstrate the importance Costa Ricans hold for education. Costa Rica has many leaders who were teachers first and then became politicians later. In 1869, Costa Rica was the first country in the world "to make education mandatory and free" (p. 96). The country spends about 28% of its budget on elementary and secondary education. One of the banners hanging in the Museo de la Paz quotes 1987 Nobel Peace Prize winner Oscar Arias Sánchez: *"Mi tierra es tierra de maestros. Por eso es tierra de paz..."* (My country is a country of teachers. For this reason, it is a country of peace...). In Costa Rica, respect for the teaching profession is well established.

3.  Costa Rica is a democratic republic, and its location between Nicaragua and Panama allows it to play an important role as broker of economic strength in the region. Without a standing army (in 1949 it gave up the army to fund its schools), Costa Rica enjoys an excellent relationship with all other Central American nations and provides a model of stability for the region. Its economy (built on the exportation of coffee and other agricultural products) is a model for developing nations. It is currently looking for more diverse means to expand the economy, with eco-tourism

and its wealth of bio-diverse products at the forefront of this expansion. Although there is poverty (35% of the population lives below the poverty line), education has been successful in eliminating "extreme" poverty, which is at 6.9% (Baker, 1999, p. 81).

4.  We were able to establish a formal cooperative arrangement with the *Universidad Nacional* in Heredia for course work, instruction, and field experiences. With its *Maestría* (Master's program in Education), the *Universidad Nacional* was an ideal candidate for collaboration.

5.  The setting provides teachers with a wide array of cultural experiences for the development of area studies units. Volcanoes, coastal lowlands, cloud and rain forests, seacoasts, modern cities, provincial towns, and remote village populations are all within reasonable traveling distance of the seminar site in Heredia. Costa Rican legends and literature (including stories for children) are a rich literary resource but are little known outside of the country.

6.  There was already an existing relationship between Costa Rica and the University of Akron. My visit in 1998 laid the groundwork for an intercultural teacher exchange in 2000 and 2001 in which teachers from Costa Rica came to Akron, Ohio, to stay with teachers and visit classes. In Costa Rica, *Intercambios Culturales* located educator families who opened their homes and classrooms to our participants.

With all these features, Costa Rica proved to be an excellent site for the teacher training and professional development program we wanted to create.

### Goals of the Program

Our program focused on helping elementary and secondary teachers of Spanish achieve the following goals: (1) increase the ability to understand and use Spanish; (2) understand the concept of culture as beliefs and values (seen in everyday life and institutions); (3) recognize patterns of interaction and behavior and strengthen intercultural competency skills; (4) know and understand historical and contemporary socio-economic and geo-political issues in Costa Rica and their influence on Costa Rica's role in Central America; (5) have knowledge of and experiences in Costa Rica's educational system; (6) make contacts for current and future intercultural cooperation; and, (7) create a teaching unit that integrates knowledge of cultural, socio-economic, and geo-political issues into working curricula.

Teachers and university students were selected based on their desire to improve their language ability and their cultural knowledge of Costa Rica, the support provided by their district or college supervisor, and their ability to express how they would incorporate knowledge gained from the seminar into their own teaching or professional situation. As a result, 22 participants spent four weeks in Costa Rica. These participants included: two PreK-8 Spanish teachers, four middle school Spanish teachers, nine secondary Spanish language teachers, three pre-service teachers, two postsecondary instructors, and two Spanish language students.

## The Academic Program in Costa Rica

The seminar took place in Heredia at the *Universidad Nacional* (UNA*)*, whose administration and staff were dedicated to providing quality instructional programs. One of the primary missions of the UNA, *"analizar ...la realidad nacional y regional"* (examine the national and regional reality), suited well our objectives for seminar participants. The UNA has a strong undergraduate and graduate teacher training program with excellent facilities available. It also provides intensive Spanish language and culture programs for non-native Spanish speakers.

During the seminar, participants attended classes that included field trips to schools, museums, parks, businesses, and historical monuments. The seminar combined a linguistic, pedagogical, cultural, and experiential focus with the intent of providing a holistic view of Costa Rican and Central American cultures. Topics explored were broad in scope: (1) the Costa Rican educational system and its policies; (2) children's literature; (3) contemporary life and society; (4) the historical, political, and cultural heritage of the people of Costa Rica; (5) the fine arts; (6) the role of eco-tourism and the role of agriculture in commerce and international trade; (7) contemporary problems of Costa Rica and Central America; and, (8) strategies for teaching Spanish as a second language. The uniqueness of Costa Rican culture and society came to life through experiences outside of the classroom. Seminar participants more easily understood contributions of the *cafetelera* society through a visit to the theater in San José that was built by the earnings of this "new" business class from the 19th century. A lecture by an economist on the cultivation and exportation of coffee was followed by a trip to Café Britt, a coffee plantation and exportation facility. Additional field trips to school sites, museums, the *Fundación de la Paz*, and a local rainforest park *(INBIO)*, all enhanced cultural learning. Rafting the Reventazón River and visiting the beautiful Sarapiquí Falls followed lectures on economics of the country and the importance of eco-tourism. A three-day excursion to Monteverde, a mountainous rainforest park, enabled participants to experience first-hand the exotic vegetation and bio-diversity of a cloud forest.

At the *Universidad Nacional,* the director of the Master's in Education Program was ideally suited to provide the instructional and logistical support to the seminar. As a result of the collaboration, our students obtained many new ideas from degree candidates who presented proficiency-based projects on teaching Spanish as a second language.

Participants found the academic part of the program to be extremely beneficial. The classes provided the concepts and theories, while the field experiences and excursions provided the link to application. Sessions on economics, which dealt with eco-tourism and current political aspects, helped participants appreciate the bigger picture of a small country of only four million people that has developed a major leadership role in Central America's peace efforts. Time spent with the Costa Rican people (*ticos*) at "home" or in public places reinforced the learning acquired through instruction. Participants said they would feel more comfortable teaching units on Costa Rica now that they have experienced living in another culture and have a "hands-on feeling about the language and people." They unanimously expressed having a "better understanding of Costa Rican mentality."

Participants liked the university classes and especially appreciated visits to elementary and secondary schools in an urban setting. They learned new concepts that did not always fit with their view and were, thus, able to compare the two cultures and reach a better understanding of how, as a world, we are interconnected and interdependent. One participant made the following observation:

> Understanding the economic effect of the trend of eating in a McDonald's restaurant on a country like Costa Rica requires knowing that growing cattle to eat hamburgers impacts the land. As a result of this eating trend, Costa Ricans are cutting down the rainforest to make more pasture land. The global effect of American customs, practices, and economy is incredible.

Another participant commented:

> We were able to see how Costa Rica has its own racial conflicts through the way Costa Ricans talked about Puerto Viejo. We see the effects of racism and the need for understanding racial issues in other countries.

Many participants were already familiar with Spain or Mexico. As a result of the seminar, all participants talked about their greater awareness of differences among Spanish-speaking countries. The one Spanish teacher who before the trip confessed she avoided teaching about Central America in her classroom gained a greater understanding of Costa Rica and its place in the world, and, consequently, she no longer evades Central America in her curriculum. Another participant stated that through his family experience he learned a great deal about what teenagers are like in other countries. Overall, participants left the summer adventure with a greater cultural understanding of Costa Rican perspectives, practices, and products.

## Homestays

At the beginning and end of the trip, participants were housed with host families selected by the *Intercambios Interculturales*. The selection of host families was based on their affiliation with schooling institutions. Akron elementary teachers were placed with Costa Rican primary teachers, Akron secondary teachers with Costa Rican secondary teachers. This experience gave our participants the opportunity to develop a common bond through discussion of professional issues while living in total immersion. Participants benefited from hearing and speaking the language through involvement in everyday Costa Rican life. While attending classes at the UNA (19 days), participants were required to stay with a host family approved by the UNA Office of International Programs. These families were not educators but offered a hospitable experience to our participants.

With one exception, everyone stated that the two homestays were the most beneficial aspect of the program. Three participants lived with school administrators and found that situation to be particularly advantageous. During the first week, most participants accompanied their host to school every day and witnessed a great number of differences between the U.S. and Costa Rican educational systems. One host was an elementary school principal who heped her semiar participant meet many other educators, writers, and heads of the educational system. Another teacher, who stayed with a high school principal, was able to participate in a national teachers' conference.

One person was able to learn about Costa Rica from two cultural perspectives because the host was a Nicaraguan national. Many host families made a special effort to bring cultural experiences into the lives of the participants and to share their knowledge of their country's history, legends, and culture. Other host families not only explained Costa Rican culture but escorted their guest on several day excursions.

A significant benefit in the homestays was that the families spoke in Spanish, thus providing the enriched linguistic environment that non-native speakers need to acquire, increase, and maintain their linguistic ability in the target language. It was not only through the interaction with the families that they learned a great deal about Costa Rica's history and culture, but through the uniqueness of the local spoken Spanish. Families enriched participants' vocabulary and their cultural understanding of region. *Cafetelera* society gained greater meaning as American teachers listened to the stories told by their *tico* hosts and, thus, acquired new *costarricense* words. For all participants, the relationship between language and culture took on new meaning.

Perhaps the greatest asset of the program was that participants were able to live in the house of an educator and "see how education is handled." Moreover, as a "family member" in an educator's home, participants were able to talk more extensively to educators about the Costa Rican educational system:

> Being with educators and speaking with other educators in Costa Rica allowed [me] to compare what [I] do with what they do.

> Being in the schools and seeing how their education works is a plus; it was a whole different world.

One major cultural discovery was that Costa Rican teachers give personal responsibility to students for their own learning, a sharp contrast with the American belief that it is the resonsibility of the teacher to motivate the child. Until this concept was explained, participants felt that Costa Rican discipline was lax. Also different was the way in which teachers dealt with instruction in schools where students number 35-40 in the classroom and where textbooks are limited. This observation gave a new perspective to teachers who feel they cannot be effective because they often have to deal with too many problems beyond the presentation of the curriculum.

## Program Requirements

As a requirement of the program, participants completed a teaching unit to be used in their own instructional setting. Examples of teaching units on Costa Rica include: legends; geography; weather and the cloud forest; health and medical procedures; the family; geology and land formation; and, nutrition. Teachers have chosen to present the units through WebQuest or picture postcards in a PowerPoint presentation. One teacher chose to create a unit based on articles from the newspaper, *La Nación*. One teacher has already developed multiple units for her classroom instruction and has been very pleased with her students' enthusiasm for the culturally-authentic content and materials. The seminar Web site is available at: <http://www.uakron.edu/lrc/fulbright/>.

## Conclusion

By spending four weeks in Costa Rica, seminar participants acquired knowledge of the contemporary cultural situation in Central America and enhanced their linguistic knowledge through formal instruction. Participants increased their proficiency through the immersion experience of homestays and daily contact with their families and other Costa Rican nationals. The seminar provided participants an opportunity to conduct research and collect data and materials for their curriculum project on the people, history, and daily life in Costa Rica. Participants overwhelmingly found they benefited most from their stay in the educator host family. As cultural investigators, they discovered the meaning of *pura vida* (a Costa Rican expression of joy that defies translation). The seminar was designed to be not only a short-term immersion experience but also a long-term partnership between elementary and secondary teachers and postsecondary students of Spanish. The relationships built will also allow teachers to continue contact with Costa Rican educators for future intercultural collaboration. The dissemination of the Costa Rican area-studies curricular units will help instructors appreciate the inherent value of integrating a wide range of cultural knowledge and activities into the curriculum. As the Hispanic population of the U.S. grows and as we forge new alliances and trade partnerships with more Central and South American countries, such knowledge is vital to our national economic and strategic objectives. Learning about Costa Rica, its culture, and its rainforest environment will help students in all levels of Spanish become enthusiastic about language studies and obtain a more balanced knowledge of Spanish language and cultures.

## References

Baker, C. (1999) *Costa Rica Handbook*. Chico, CA: Moon Publishers.

Gorka, B. & Niesenbaum, R. (2001). Beyond the language requirement: Interdisciplinary short-term study-abroad programs in Spanish. *Hispania, 84* (1), 100-108.

Schumann, J. (1976a). Social distance as a factor in second language acquisition. *Language Learning, 26* (1), 135-143.

Schumann, J. (1976b). Second language acquisition: The pidginization hypothesis. *Language Learning, 26* (2), 391-408.

## Suggested Readings

Coleman, J. A. (1995). Residence abroad within language study. *Language Teaching, 30* (1), 1-20.

Freed, B. (1995). What makes us think that students who study abroad become fluent? In B. Freed (Ed.), *Second language acquisition in a study abroad context* (pp. 123-148). Amsterdam and Philadelphia: John Benjamins Publishing.

Freed, B. (1998). An overview of issues and research in language learning in a study abroad setting. *Frontiers: The Interdisciplinary Journal of Study Abroad IV*, 31-60.

Gardner, R. & Lambert, W. (1972). *Attitudes and motivation in second-language learning*. Rowley, MA: Newbury House Publishers.

Lapking, S., Hart, D., & Swain, M. (1995). A Canadian interprovincial exchange: Evaluating the linguistic impact of a three-month stay in Quebec. In B. Freed (Ed.), *Second language acquisition in a study abroad context* (pp. 67-94). Amsterdam and Philadelphia: John Benjamins Publishing.

Lutz, K. (2001). Notes from a traveler to Costa Rica: ¡Pura vida! *The Cardinal: Newsletter of the Ohio Foreign Language Association, 40* (2), 10-11.